Mary Slessor

WOMEN OF FAITH

Mary Slessor

HEROINE OF CALABAR

Basil Miller

BETHANY HOUSE PUBLISHERS
MINNEAPOLIS, MINNESOTA 55438
A Division of Bethany Fellowship, Inc.

Mary Slessor: Heroine of Calabar
Basil Miller

Library of Congress Catalog Card Number 85-71477

ISBN 0-87123-849-7

Published by Bethany House Publishers
A Division of Bethany Fellowship, Inc.
6820 Auto Club Road, Minneapolis, Minnesota 55438

Printed in the United States of America

CONTENTS

WOMEN OF FAITH SERIES

Amy Carmichael
Corrie ten Boom
Florence Nightingale
Gladys Aylward
Hannah Whitall Smith
Isobel Kuhn
Mary Slessor
Joni

MEN OF FAITH SERIES

Borden of Yale
Brother Andrew
C. S. Lewis
Charles Finney
Charles Spurgeon
Eric Liddell
George Muller
Hudson Taylor
Jim Elliot
Jonathan Goforth
John Hyde
John Wesley
Martin Luther
Samuel Morris
Terry Waite
William Carey
William Booth
D. L. Moody

John and Betty Stam

CHAPTER 1

THE DREAM THAT CAME TRUE

Mary Slessor was a born missionary. From her earliest days no dream burned in her soul save this, and Calabar to which she was destined to go was written on her heart. Mary was always a missionary. When she played with her dolls, she imagined they were tiny babies whose black mothers had given them birth in faraway Calabar. In the fancyland of make-believe, with sticks for pupils, she taught Sunday school, but always that teaching was in the dark heart of West Africa.

As a child she breathed the spiritual air of Calabar, and in the coming decades grateful generations were to honor her with the surname of that heathen country, so that today she is known as Mary Slessor *of Calabar*. In her childhood she was passionately wedded to that land, and she sought no other career, no other love, save the joy of carrying the glorious Gospel of salvation to Calabar's blacks. This affection was second only to her adoration of Christ, who had washed her in His redeeming blood.

Her mind fed upon Calabar during her turbulent youth, and her soul burned with the desire to seek the Master's lost sheep of this her adopted land. She was inspired by this one motive: to present her Lord with Calabar as a trophy of His transforming grace. Mary was a mill girl, a weaver, like her fellow Scotsman, Livingstone, but the twelve-hour shift at the mill each day was part of the preparation for her great trek to Africa.

She dreamed of Calabar, and the Master made her dreams tangible realities.

In the early sixties of the last century the people of Dun-

dee, Scotland, saw on its streets a girl with burning blue
eyes and a shock of curly red hair. Her mouth was firm,
denoting determination, and her complexion was as fresh
as a dewy rose petal. The slim Scottish girl carried a dinner pail for she was on her way to the mill, where she
spent long hours at the shuttles.

She walked with a tripping step, for she glowed with a
buoyant spirit of hope. She was in love with life and
touched with compassion for humanity. Mary was young,
but her sincerity attracted people then as later when she was
to be graced with the title of "The White Queen of Okoyong." Ostensibly on her way to the mill, in reality she
was already in the wilds of Africa, where she was to acquire
fame, almost the match of Livingstone's, for a beneficent
life spent in winning a forgotten people for her Master.

This was young Mary Slessor, already burdened with
trouble and loaded with grief, for hers was to be a life
purified in the crucible of trial. Aberdeen was her birth-
place, and that cold December 2, 1848, on which she was
born matches in majesty the birthdate of the world's greatest heroines. Her father, Robert, was a drinking shoemaker,
who did as much for Mary by dying early as by any other
act of his career.

Mother Slessor was marked with piety, and gave little
Mary, and her older brother, Robert, a plain and generous
home, graced with an air of refinement, for she herself was
the only child of moderately wealthy, religious parents.
Her gentleness and retiring disposition, her interest in
church activities and her vital concern for missions—especially Calabar—did much to influence little Mary.

Foremost in her thoughts, even when the family circle
included only Robert and baby Mary, was the West Coast
of Africa, particularly dark Calabar. She told many strange
and weird stories to Mary and Robert—stories filled with

the trials and triumphs of Christ's missionaries in that mysterious land.

The children—Robert, Mary, Susan, John, down to the seventh, Janie—listened wide-eyed, and often the oldest, Robert, then a little man who was to set a spark ablaze in his sister's heart, boldly proclaimed to the family circle that *he* was going to be a missionary when he grew to be a big, big, *big* man!

Looking at his whimpering sister, Mary, he said, "And when I am a missionary, I'll take you to the pulpit with me." This consoled her childish heart, and no schoolteacher was more conscientious than Mary as she told the old, old story of love and redemption to her dolls—the dark-skinned children of Calabar.

Mary was then a missionary, but far away from the land of her heart. This childish dream of Calabar was a dim light on time's distant horizon. The father gave himself wholly to drink, and the family fortunes fell steadily, until finally, in 1859, when Mary was eleven, the Slessors moved from their native hearth and found an abode in Dundee, which henceforth was to be the family home. The hope that new surroundings might help to break Father Robert's drink habit was not to be realized, but the industrial town afforded opportunities for work.

Dark days clouded the Slessor household, and when the seventh child, Janie, came, the money from the sale of their furniture in Aberdeen slowly melted away. In a bare but clean house, the delicate mother drew her children around her knee, and, opening the family Bible, read the stories of Jesus and His power to redeem. She determined that, though they were poor in earthly goods, her children were to be rich in the treasures of God's Word.

Each Sunday, as the trouble-filled weeks passed, the children, faithfully scrubbed, dressed in their best clothes, and with perfume on their handkerchiefs and peppermints in their pockets, were sent to church and Sunday school.

Those horror-marked days became months, and one by one the little Slessors were carried out to the neighboring church's cemetery, until only Mary, Susan, John and Janie were left.

Money became so scarce that the mother worked in the mills, which placed the responsibility of the household duties upon Mary's shoulders. Still the income was not sufficient to match the needs, and when Mary was eleven, she, too, went to the weaving mills as a breadwinner.

Those were times of tragedy, when even Mary's pittance added to Mother Slessor's wage was not sufficient to support the family. With tears in her eyes—tears of gladness —Mary gave her first earnings to her mother, whose eyes also brimmed at the thought of her daughter's bleak childhood in comparison with her own girlhood days in a refined home with an abundance of comforts.

The days were long and hard for Mary, and from six in the morning until six in the evening she tended the shuttles, from her eleventh to her fourteenth year. Dark and dank were the weaving sheds, where she watched the whirring belts, the clacking looms, the darting shuttles. The deafening din was distressing, but Mary, like young David decades earlier, placed a book before her, and when time permitted she read. She must be studious, she knew, if she were to be a missionary.

At times the dream seemed to disappear, but when she reached home she would recapture the vision by reading a book borrowed from the Sunday school library or a friend. Mary read such serious books as *Paradise Lost* and *Sartor Resartus,* lent her by a friend, who thought Mary somewhat young for such dull and heavy reading.

"How did you get on with Carlyle?" he teasingly asked her.

"He's grand," she replied enthusiastically. "I sat reading it and never knew what time it was till I heard the factory bells in the morning."

The Bible was her favorite. In later years this Book inspired her to greater achievements than her contemporaries thought possible, and marked her writing with a beauty of style and power of diction which were evident in the spiritual fervor of her writings regarding missions.

Once, when asked by a girl for something to read, Mary said, handing her a Bible, "Take that; it has made me a changed lassie."

The drinking father edged nearer the precipice, and one by one the family possessions were sold. When Mary returned from work, she was met at the door by her mother, who handed her a wrapped bundle, which Mary rushed to the pawnbroker. With the money clutched tightly in her hand, she hurried home, so that once again the family might eat. The smile of relief, circling her mother's face, brought gladness to her.

Often her father became abusive, and one night Mary was forced to flee to escape him. There were tears in her eyes, a prayer in her heart, and her spirit was heavy with grief. Saturday nights were the worst. After the younger children had been put to bed, Mary and her downcast mother waited for the father's uncertain steps. Often when the drunken father came home, he threw into the fire the food of which the rest of the family had deprived themselves that he might eat.

Mary, however, had a growing source of sustenance in her religious life. On moving to Dundee, Mother Slessor took the children to the Wishart Church, named for the noted preacher, George Wishart, who in 1544 had preached near the site shortly before being martyred. Mary found a place in the Sunday school and when service time came she was always present. However, at this time she did not take her religion seriously and speaks of herself as "a wild lassie."

She and her playmates enjoyed knocking on doors and running away to watch the householders as they sought the source of the knocks. In staid and strict Scotland of a hundred years ago such conduct on the part of a girl was considered a mad prank.

The bold independence of custom and defiance of conventionality which was later to characterize her was beginning to assert itself. Mary was never strait-jacketed by custom. Despite these escapades, the preaching and Sunday school teaching deeply touched her life, and she went to her mother with questions which showed serious thought regarding her soul's welfare.

"Is baptism necessary for salvation?" she once asked, an earnestness coming into her eyes. "Well," replied the mother, who had traveled the soul-road that leads to forgiveness and redemption, but who knew a girl's heart, "the Bible says he that repents and is baptized shall be saved. But it does not say that he who repents and is not baptized shall be damned."

At another time when her daughter asked about duty, wise Mother Slessor told her, "When one duty jostles another, one is not a duty." Mary could never forget her mother's advice when she said:

"Thank God for what you receive. Thank God for what you do not receive. Thank God for the sins you are delivered from, and thank God for the sins that you know nothing about and are never tempted to commit."

Mother Slessor thus became her daughter's tutor in religious matters and helped open to Mary the doors of

salvation by introducing her to the wonderful truths of
the Bible. Mary read the Word and learned to love it
deeply, even before she became a Christian. God was
calling the young girl, and shortly an incident took place
which turned her thoughts to Him.

Near by lived a widow, deeply interested in the young
girls of the community, who was concerned about their
salvation. She often called them into her home and spoke
with them about their souls. One cold winter day, she
invited Mary and several other girls into her house and
spoke to them about the fire. Then she cleverly shifted
the conversation to temptation and sin.

"Do you see that fire? If you put your hand into the
flames," she said in broad Scottish, "it would be very bad.
It would burn you. But if ye dinna repent 'n' believe on
the Lord Jesus Christ, your soul will burn in the lowin',
blazin' fire forever and ever."

Terror struck Mary's heart. She could not escape the
awful thought of eternal punishment. She felt that she
must find a refuge in Jesus, a safety from the fires of doom.
At once she knew that she must entrust herself to Christ's
keeping and be saved. The glorious light of redemption
burst upon her heart which had been convicted of sin, and
casting her soul upon the Lord's mercy, she was converted.

This was a happy occasion for Mother Slessor, and when
Mary told her, together they rejoiced in the goodness of
God. The mother knew now that her daughter was safe in
God's kingdom. Little did she dream of the great work
the Master had for her to accomplish, but whatever the
tomorrows, wherever the hand of God should lead, she was
willing for her Mary to walk in duty's path.

At once the weaving lassie took up church work with
a sense of spiritual determination to win others to the
Christ who had saved her. She asked the superintendent

of the Sunday school for a class to teach, and was given what
she termed a group of "lovable lassies."   Looking back upon
those early teaching days, she characterized them as being
filled with "the impudence of ignorance in a special degree."

She had a reservoir of love for Christ.   Out of a heart filled
with spiritual radiance overflowed a compassion which
drew people to her, and through her, to the Master.

Wishart Church was in the slums, in a section where
streets were narrow and the passages which led from
them were called Pends.   Here the Pends led from the
main streets into the poverty-stricken tenement sections.
From these dreary and sunless buildings came a crowd of
rough, undisciplined boys and girls who played in the
streets.

As Mary went back and forth to the factory and to the
various church meetings, her heart ached for these children.   She wanted to bring them under the influence of
the church and teach them that Jesus could set joybells
ringing in their hearts as He had done in hers.   Finally,
when a mission was opened near the worst of the Pends, she
volunteered as a teacher.   But the superintendent, looking
at the slight girl, decided that she would be unable to dis-
cipline the ruffians with whom she must deal.

But the radiance which burst from her cleansed heart
glowed in her face.   Her assurance of having been born
again touched the superintendent, and consequently **Mary**
was given a class to teach.

The ruffians often tried to disrupt the services, but Mary
went to the streets in an endeavor to win the young people.
One lad in particular was vexing, and shouted, "If you don't
leave us alone, we will hurt you."   Mary faced them with
a prayer for courage, and said, "I will not give up the
work.   Do whatever you like."

"Here goes," shouted the leader, taking a piece of string

from his pocket to which a weight was tied. He started to whirl it above his head, coming closer each time to Mary's face. But she did not flinch as the gang watched breathlessly. Finally as it grazed her forehead, the bully dropped the weight to the ground.

"We can't scare her, boys," he said. "She's game," he added, turning to face the girl whose glowing smile had touched his heart. Mary asked them to come to the services, and several of them followed her.

Another boy with a whip in his hand often challenged Mary at the mission door. One night the little home missionary said, "Suppose we changed places, what would happen?"

"I would get this whip across my shoulders," he said, to which Mary replied, "I will bear it for you, if you'll go in."

When he asked if she really meant it, Mary told him to apply the whip to her. Throwing the whip to the ground, he was conquered by love and followed her into the mission.

Often Mary took her class into the country where she told them about nature and introduced them to nature's God. Nor was she afraid to visit them in their homes. Going into these slum homes, she took her practical religion with her, and when a baby needed tending, she served as nurse. Always Mary told the family about Christ and His power to save, and as she drank tea out of a broken cup or ate from an unwashed plate, she fitted herself into the family group.

It was this ability to mingle with these slum folk which prepared her for mission work. This service for her Saviour lightened the drudgery of her twelve-hour shifts in the factory. In spite of her long hours, the recreation she found in Christian work kept her heart filled with gladness. She was happy, a carefree girl, to whom God was a living Person, a close Friend, upon whom she could cast her burdens. Many they were indeed. Jesus was closer than even her dear mother, and His love, tender compassion and tragic death for her sins put a desire in her soul which drove her to Africa to live and die that others might know Him.

Never once during those years did the missionary enthusiasm flicker in the Slessor household. When missionaries came to the Wishart Church or to Dundee, Mary and her mother always went to hear them. Feeding her soul on the spiritual works of such men as Doddridge and Baxter, Mary was emboldened to ask God to make it possible for her to cross the sea and become His missionary.

Meanwhile Robert, the missionary-to-be, died, and this left only John, the youngest son, whom Mother Slessor had hoped would be a missionary. But God had other plans. John sickened and was sent to New Zealand for his health, only to die on arrival, and again the Scottish home in Dundee was grief-stricken.

Reading missionary books and missionary magazines which told of spiritual treks in China, Africa, Japan and even Calabar, Mary one day saw a great light, which flared forth on the horizon of her soul, and she asked herself, *Why don't I become a missionary?*

Working at the looms, she considered the idea. As she walked to and from work she challenged herself with the thought. On her knees she recalled all she had heard about dear Calabar. She laid the problem before the Lord. There were the tropical jungles, the black people, the wild animals, death, destruction, devastation.

Black men without God and without hope!

Brightly the vision came to her, and she saw herself as their teacher, the sent-one who should carry redemption's story to their benighted souls. On her knees she consecrated herself to the task. She would do it. She was God's, and the Master had commanded her to carry the Gospel to the uttermost parts of the earth, even to Calabar.

It was 1874, and Mary was twenty-six. Somewhere in lonely Africa a brave Scot was on his knees, his head in his hands. He had said "good-bye" to this world and had been welcomed to that bright land of everlasting day. The message went throughout the world and to Dundee:

Livingstone is dead!

The decision was made. Mary went to her mother with her story.

"I want to offer myself as a missionary. Are you willing?"

"Gladly I am," said Mother Slessor. "You'll make a fine missionary." With this prayer about to be answered, a prayer the mother had prayed since the birth of her first son, Robert, tears of joy leaped from the mother's eyes and splashed down her cheeks. There was to be a missionary in the family!

Others shook their heads in doubt, but armed with her mother's blessing, this brave Scot could not be daunted. Her sisters, Susan and Janie, were both working and well able to support their mother, so Mary's last burden was removed.

The following year, 1875, she offered herself to the Foreign Mission Board of her church, the United Presbyterian, and asked to be sent to Calabar. Her church had always considered the work of missions to be primary, and it was not an uncommon thing for them to accept a woman for this service. Mary's heart tingled as she waited for the reply, which came early in 1876, and stated that she was appointed as a teacher to Calabar and was to continue her studies at Dundee. But in March of that year, it was decided that she should spend three months at an Edinburgh normal school.

Her last words on leaving the home city were: *"Pray for me."* She realized that for these long years, since childhood days, she had depended upon prayer, and now, without the arm of man upon which to lean, she must continue to pray.

When told at the school that Calabar was "the white man's grave," Mary said, "But it is also a post of honor. Since few volunteer for that section, I wish to go because my Master needs me there." One of her friends tells us that as Mary spoke, her face was radiant with a heavenly glow, showing clearly to all who saw her that Christ dwelt within.

Finally, school preparation over, on August 5, 1876, she went to Liverpool, from where, on the S. S. *Ethiopia,* she sailed for Calabar, the land of her dreams. For fourteen long years she had worked at the looms, but while working she had dreamed of being in Calabar's dark regions, teaching, preaching, winning benighted souls to the Master.

Now that dream had come true. Robert, who was to take her to the pulpit with him, had long since been laid to rest, but the vision he had helped to give to his sister Mary never dimmed, and she, feeling that she must carry a double load—hers as well as his—looked into the Master's face, pledged herself anew to His service, and sailed away for the land of her heart's delight.

When the gangplank was up, Mary, looking about her, saw the evidence of Africa's degradation and its cause. She said, "Scores of casks: but only one missionary." England, her native land, faded from sight, but ever looming larger in her vision was Calabar, her adopted homeland.

Chapter 2

CALABAR'S JUNGLE LAND

Mary's heart rejoiced as the ship cut the waters southward and four weeks passed. She was sailing from the cold gray skies of the north into the warmth and brilliance of tropical seas. The great open expanse about her, the majesty of the ocean were a welcome change from Dundee's narrow streets, throbbing with life. Her spirits lifted, and the young Scottish woman reveled in the joy of a mission soon to be fulfilled.

She became a favorite on the ship, for the passengers were attracted to the bright, kindly girl, though they shook their heads pessimistically when they talked of the region to which she was going and the jungles she was seeking to conquer. On board was a Mr. Thomson, who, with his wife, was going to Calabar. He was an architect who dreamed of the possibility of establishing a retreat where the worn missionaries might come to rest and rebuild their tired bodies. He had previously explored the West Coast and selected the Cameroon Mountains, and he was now on his way to build a home for mission workers there.

He told Mary about the wonders of this strange country to which she was traveling; he described its dense mud-colored rivers with their lush green banks. The sun was fierce, the animals wild and the tornadoes terrific, he said. The picture was not pleasant despite the fact that the architect spoke of the brilliant flowers and bright birds. It took more than a lurid description of dangers to daunt Mary. A glorious purpose drove her on, and difficulties but tightened the reins of her spirit. She was on a soul trek which was to be the grandest journey anyone had ever taken.

Finally, on September 11, the steamer turned landward
and entered the turbulent waters of the Cross and Calabar
Rivers, which here poured into the sea. Mary long before
had become acquainted with these rivers. There were
gloomy swamps, dark and impenetrable. Cranes and peli-
cans moved lazily as the steamer came near, and ferocious
man-eating crocodiles slid off sandbanks into the brackish
waters.

Soon she spied the clay cliffs and the mud dwellings,
thatched with palm leaves which quivered in the wind.
Native canoes skimmed out to the steamer, followed by
boats of traders and missionaries. Duke Town, her first
African home, was reached and though torrid in the sun,
mud-coated and rude, still to her it was the grandest sight
this side of the Heavenly City.

High on a hill above the town was the mission home,
where she first met "Daddy and Mammy Anderson," as
they were called, pioneer missionaries of her church. Mammy Anderson set Mary to work immediately and one of her
first duties was to ring the rising bell for morning prayers.
Often she overslept, unmindful of the short night hours she
had spent as a Dundee mill lassie, and more than once, on
awaking and finding the earth drenched with light, she
pulled the bell rope with strong muscles. Much to her
amazement she discovered, when one of the workers rebelled against being summoned to prayer much too early,
that the light was from a brilliant tropical moon and not
the dawn-breaking sun.

Mary was delighted with the novelty of her new work,
and in eager enjoyment she took long walks into the bush
with the children. She was thrilled by exotic plants, bril-
liantly plumaged birds, flaming sunsets and nights made
weird with jungle calls. Often she wrote poetry:

> . . . the shimmering, dancing wavelets
> And the stately, solemn palms,
> The wild, weird chant of the boatman
> And the natives' evening psalms,
> The noise of myriad insects
> And the firefly's soft, bright sheen,
> The bush with its thousand terrors
> And its never fading green.

She ran races with the black children, thus winning their confidence. She climbed trees like a boy, in an endeavor to recapture her own lost childhood. Many times she said she had climbed every tree for miles around. These exploits made her late for meals and called the tender wrath of Mrs. Anderson upon her. She would be sent to her room without food, only to have Daddy bring biscuits and bananas smuggled to her with Mammy's consent.

Mary never forgot her great mission. She had come to Africa to win souls, teach boys and girls about Jesus, and she earnestly assumed her new duties. The mission staff was small and their labors were confined chiefly to Duke Town, Old Town and Creek Town, three towns at the Calabar River's mouth. The work was thirty years old, and the missionaries had ventured to open two outstations at Ikunetu and Ikorofiong on Cross River.

Beyond this was the unexplored wilderness, filled with people enslaved by revolting customs. There Mary longed to be, but for the present she must content herself with work in the Calabar district. She knew that here an example of Christ's transforming power must be shown the natives which in time would open the untouched jungles to the Gospel. Mary knew that old customs must be broken and a new way of life instituted—a way of life by which the converted natives could live. Truth must be taught, but more than this, the Truth must be *lived*.

Wanting to accomplish results quickly, she adopted the motto, "Learn of me." Then she remembered that someone had said, "Jesus was never in a hurry," so she slowed her pace and methodically went about her duties.

At first she taught in the day school on Mission Hill, and then she visited the yards or compounds in Duke Town. Often she took trips to the outlying stations. Wherever she went, whatever she was doing, Jesus was her theme, and His love for dying humanity was her compelling motive.

Once while she was making a trip the children ran from her in fright, for they had never seen a white "Ma," a term in the Efik language used to indicate respect for a woman. Loving children as she did, this cut her to the heart, but soon she became the honored white Ma of a growing district.

On one of these trips she gave her first Gospel message to the natives. The missionary with whom she traveled finished her talk and then turned to Mary, asking her to speak. Her moment had at last arrived, and, asking her fellow missionary to read a few verses from the wonderful Bible, Mary began in simple language to tell the people of Jesus' saving and transforming power. She spoke of the joy His coming into their lives would bring and the hope of life beyond death.

The natives listened intently, deeply impressed, and henceforth when the white Ma visited the district, they came in crowds to see her and hear the wonderful stories which she told them.

These were not easy trips for her to take, for they necessitated fatiguing marches through the bush, hill-climbing, jumping fallen trees, wading deep streams and enduring drenching rains, even tornadoes. These difficulties were not of vital concern to Mary. Her one thought was to tell the story of Jesus to the people in their homes and compounds. Here she met heathenism at its worst.

Beneath the beauty of birds and blossoms and brilliant

sunsets were superstitions, cruelty, suffering and belief in repulsive gods. She saw the natives' lives burdened and ordered by cruel, merciless and autocratic rules. She learned that the head of each community, often a cluster of mud huts in the bush, was the chief. He ruled with many wives and slaves over whom he exercised the authority of life and death.

A secret society, known as Egbo, flourished, and the Egbo runners struck terror to the natives when they appeared from the bush. Attired in alarming garb, they rushed into the villages and along the forest paths, lashing with long whips and committing various offenses against the people. Mary saw the drinking and the terrible traffic in slaves. Misery and degradation were everywhere.

She had, however, a sustaining power, the glory and presence of the Lord Jesus, whose servant she was, and who was able to tame the wild beasts in the natives' hearts.

"Ah, lassie," said Mammy Anderson to Mary when she had spoken about what she had seen on a bush trip, "you haven't seen anything yet. In the bush and far back in the interior are millions of these black people. Most of them are slaves. They can be sold, whipped or killed . . . The tribes are wild and cruel. They pass their lives in fighting, dancing and drinking.

"Many are cannibals. When a chief dies, his wives and slaves have their heads cut off and are buried with him. A slave receives no more consideration than a pig. They sleep on the ground like animals, and are branded with a hot iron. Many have their ears cut off, and the girls are fattened like animals and sold for slave wives."

Pausing awhile for Mary to grasp the full significance of what she was saying, Mother Anderson added, "And one of the worst customs is the treatment of twins."

"What is that?" asked the bonnie lass from Dundee.

"The people fear twins worse than death," continued the veteran missionary. "They are not allowed to live. They are killed, crushed into pots and thrown into the bush. The mother is also driven out. No one will have anything to do with her, leaving her to die in the forests or be eaten by the animals."

Mary's eyes filled with horror, as she thought of her own love for babies and Jesus' call to "suffer the little children to come unto me and forbid them not . . . "

"I shall fight this," she said vehemently with all the fire of her Scottish soul. "It must be stopped . . . I will never give up."

The youthful missionary took on the most difficult task of her career. She was determined to die or save the twin babies and break this terrible custom. Realizing the enormity of her task, she said, "There is much work to be done. I must learn the language so that we can understand each other better."

At once she began the study of Efik, the Calabarian language of trade and commerce, spoken in a wide neighboring district. Soon she mastered the difficulties and intricacies of this tongue, and added another link in the chain which drew people to her. Now she was able to teach the little black scholars in their own language as she had done in her imagination in those far-off Scottish days when she played with her dolls and imagined them to be black children.

Going about her duties, she made many friends, supreme among whom was a chief at Creek Town, King Eyo Honesty VII. Hearing him speak, she was impressed by his simplicity and earnestness, and on learning that it was he about whom the missionaries had told her mother in Dundee, she spoke to the king about it. As a result, for many years letters were exchanged by the dark Christianized chief in Africa and the delicate little Christian mother in Scotland. In the same town was a Mrs. Fuller, a colored woman who had come as a nurse with earlier missionaries. She had married and now lived at the mission house. A kindly, unselfish soul, she was a favorite in the town and instantly took a warm liking to the young lady from Scotland.

"I believe you would say a good word about the devil himself," Mary told the colored woman.

"Well," returned the nurse, "at any rate, he minds his own business."

Many were the daily visits Mary made to the Duke Town yards, so that she could keep in touch with the natives in their homes. Thus she discovered by this means the powerful chains with which the superstitions had bound them. During one such Sunday visit she saw an old man sitting disconsolately at his hut's door.

"Why are you not on your way to God's house?" she asked quietly. "Mr. Anderson will expect you."

"If your heart was sad, would you go to any place?" the old man asked. Upon inquiry Mary learned that his only child had died and "even now is buried in the house."

Mary's heart welled within her and she told the sorrow-bowed black the marvelous story of Lazarus' resurrection from the tomb. She told of Jesus' message to Mary and Martha after their brother had died. Reading from the Bible the story of Lazarus, the young missionary tried to bring the Gospel's comfort to the man and his wife.

Before leaving she saw the light of hope in their darkened eyes, when they learned that God had taken their little child. Said the father, "Well, if God has taken him, it is not so bad."

Many of the compounds or yards she visited were crowded with women herded like animals into pens. Some

of them were being fattened for future husbands. Sensitive
Mary was shocked by this animalism. As she went from
yard to yard and saw these deplorable conditions, she
prayed that the Heavenly Father might enable her to
change this with the Gospel's transforming power.

In spite of the encouraging results the mission had experienced in Duke Town, she often came into homes which
were untouched by Christianizing influences. In one of
these she found the chief dead and the mistress, a repulsive
old woman, counting coins. Strewn everywhere were human skulls and charms, the evidences of heathen sacrifices
and cannibalism. Several half-starved women were quar-
reling over a pipe.

Ma, as she was affectionately known far and near, told
them the story of Jesus, lovingly, tenderly; she told how
He went about doing good and that He had come to bring
salvation to them. However, she accomplished little, and
was forced to leave the matter in God's hands.

Many of these homes were hovels, where pools of stag-
nant water and piles of filth and human excreta filled the
compound with sickening odors. Starvation showed
through the pinched faces, and the almost naked bodies
were covered with sores.

In one such hut an old woman shrieked, "I have prayed
and prayed and God does not answer." This gave the white
Ma an opportunity to tell her about the true and living God
who hears the cries of His children.

Often the enormity of the task appalled Mary, as she saw
the harvest, plenteous and ripe, and realized that the laborers were few. With a strong faith she overcame a tendency
to doubt the missionaries' ability to cope with the situation,
and she was confident that the battle was not theirs but the
Lord's. Steadily she went about her tasks for three years,

and faithfully she carried the Gospel sunshine into homes and hearts.

As the third year drew to a close, the trying experiences of the harsh climate weakened her physique. There were two seasons, each trying enough in itself but deadly when combined. There was the rainy season, lasting from March to December, followed by the hot and torrid weather which filled the remaining months of the year.

The latter brought the "smokes," a dull, dry haze of dust which blew in from the great African desert northward. It seemed to suck all energy from Mary's usually buoyant body. At such times she felt that her fire and vigor were gone, but she struggled on, supported by her faith in God. Attacks of ague and fever often left her semiconscious.

"Calabar needs a brave heart," she wrote to a Scotland friend, "and a stout body; not that I have very much of the former, but I have felt the need of it often when sick and lonely."

Sickness made her wish for home, and the fog and chill of Dundee. She longed for her mother and sisters, the gray skies and the tang of Scottish air. Moreover, her first furlough was due, after the trying three-year term spent in mastering the language and learning to bring cheer through the Gospel to lonely and desolate hearts. Her soul was filled with the prospect of the tremendous work to be done for the Master in this golden-ripe West Coast of Africa. She was not discouraged, but merely tired and worn.

It was a joyful letter that brought news of her furlough, and in June, 1879, in her thirty-first year, Mary stood on the deck of a homeward-bound steamer. She looked back upon the faces of her dusky friends who lined the river's bank, and watched as they waved their white Ma good-bye. Many of them cried tears of joy because she had brought the light of Christ into their hearts and homes.

She was not a defeated missionary, but merely a weary one, and after a rest at home, where she could revel in Mother Slessor's cooking and enjoy fellowship with her praying friends, she would be ready to return to Calabar.

CHAPTER 3

ADVENTURING FOR GOD IN THE JUNGLES

Mary was homeward-bound! Her heart rang with gratitude to God for permitting her to have a part in Calabar's redemption. She had found the homeland of her soul, and could never long be content away from it. The ocean voyage thrilled her body, tinted her cheeks, and gave her time for prayer, when she held before the Throne of Grace the black jewels which she hoped to win for the Master.

Arriving home, she was eagerly welcomed to the Dundee fireside, and wherever she went with the message of Calabar, she electrified the people, Mother Slessor no less than others. She had left Scotland lighthearted and filled with romantic thoughts of missionary adventure. She returned saddened by the natives' plight, matured by her constant grappling with problems beyond her ability to solve, and thoroughly consecrated to this lifelong work of bringing Christ the Saviour to dark Calabar.

In speaking to the people, she described vividly the heathen customs to be conquered, but she also told of the one remedy: Jesus' transforming power and the availability of spiritual resources for the task. Speaking as she had occasion to do at Wishart Church and elsewhere, she won friends for Calabar and inspired the prayer-warrior of her home, Mother Slessor, whom she found more spiritually minded than ever and eagerly willing to carry her share of Calabar's burdens.

Her mother's health was poor, so Mary discovered a village home at Downfield, skirting Dundee, where she moved the family. Here were the open skies and pleasant fields, where Mary's mother and two sisters were to find new enjoyment in life.

The burden of Mary's message, while she recuperated in the homeland, was her strong desire to move upward and possess the unworked fields, particularly Okoyong. For more than a year she lingered amid the familiar scenes of Dundee, but her heart was in the jungles of dark Africa to which she had dedicated her soul.

The time of her return came soon, and in October, 1880, in the company of two pioneer workers of the mission, the Rev. and Mrs. Hugh Goldie, she again set sail for Calabar. Her heart throbbed with the desire to have a station of her own, beyond Duke Town and Old Town, where the Gospel message had never been heard. She wanted to build where Christ's heralds had not yet set foot.

On arriving, she found good news awaiting her; she had been appointed to take charge of the Old Town Station, two miles up the river from her first field of work. At last she was a missionary in her own right! The difficulties she faced meant little to Mary, many and vexing though they were. On entering the town, she saw first a human skull, dangling from a pole's end as it swung lazily in the tropical breeze. The mission house was a dilapidated hut, built of wattle and mud, thatched with palm fronds. Despite its outward severity, she found the inside whitewashed and somewhat clean.

All this was inconsequential, in view of the fact that she was edging nearer the trackless jungles. Here she could wage the battle against sin, ignorance, superstition and spiritual degradation in her own way. She adopted the native mode of life, which enabled her to live less expensively than at Duke Town, thus making it possible to send a larger portion of her salary to the Scotland household. Finally she even ate native foods, luscious yams and plantains, a bananalike fruit, though less sweet and more starchy than its sister edible.

Here she was establishing habits of inestimable value for the time when in the wilder and more inaccessible fever-ridden jungle districts she would be forced to "go native" to the fullest extent.

She visited the outlying sections of Old Town where kindly hands beckoned her to the settlements as she brought the message of Jesus to sin-blackened hearts. Here she conducted a day school and held Sunday services. At one such place, mingling with young and old alike, was the king of the region, who sat on a bench with the little children.

Mary's kindly spoken words and winning manner helped to break down opposition to this new Jesus Way. Word spread rapidly of the white Ma who was telling of Jesus, the Saviour of blacks and whites alike, and from afar the natives came to attend her classes and visit her home that they might learn more about the Man of Galilee.

Mary was greatly disturbed by the heathen custom of murdering twins, which she had earlier resolved to oppose vigorously.

She discovered that the practice was based on the belief that the father of one of the twins was an evil spirit. However, no one knew which twin's father was an evil spirit, and therefore both were doomed to death. The mother, supposedly involved in this grievous devil-relationship, was likewise banished. Immediately after their birth, twins had their backs broken, and their little black bodies were stuffed in a calabash jar and thrown into the bush. Here they were eaten by wild animals or left to rot.

Twins could not be carried through the door, but must be taken from the home through a cut in the dwelling's rear, which was immediately closed after they were removed. The banished mother was left either to die of starvation in the bush or be eaten alive by fierce jungle animals.

Mary threw herself into the fight against this practice, and after much prayer she explained the wickedness of the custom and told the natives of Jesus' love for children. To show that twins were not dangerous, she determined to bring a pair to the mission house before they were mangled. She found the twins and nursed them to health, and at first the natives looked with suspicion on the Ma, believing that she was allied with a devil, but when they saw that she suffered no evil effects, gradually the superstition began to fade. Everywhere Mary became known as "the white Ma who loves babies."

One day a Scottish trader came with a black infant in his arms, saying, "It is a twin I found in the bush. The other was killed. It soon would have died, but I know how you feel about these little ones, so I brought it to you."

Taking the wee infant in her arms, she said gently, "Thank you. I'll call her Janie, after my sister." Thus Janie came into Mary's life and became one of her greatest comforts.

Life was cheap, and the children of slaves who died were also killed. "Why bother with them?" asked the natives. The missionaries began to rescue these foundlings. Mary saw that she would not have energy to carry on this rescue work, so she suggested to the Mission Board that a special worker be appointed for this task.

The injustice of another practice aroused her fighting spirit. The tribe that had settled on the Coast previously had been permitted to do so through the generosity of the black men who formerly occupied the region. But when they had secured a foothold, the interlopers would not permit the original tribe to bring their nuts, palm oil and other products to the trade marts. Fights ensued, and blood was shed as the sentries found the tribesmen coming in.

Mary saw the injustice of this, and gradually began to

help smuggle the backland traders and their wares into the town. When the upriver men came in, she led them by a path through the mission to the near-by trading posts, where their business was conducted. The European traders, of course, welcomed the missionary's assistance, and in turn the outlanders obtained supplies and her co-operation helped to establish a spirit of good will.

These Christian labors had their effect, and Daddy Anderson, in the neighboring station, praised Mary before the Mission Board. When in 1881-82, home deputies came on a tour of inspection, they were impressed by her boundless energy, sincere devotion to duty and Christian zeal.

"Her labors are manifold," they reported to the home Board, "but she sustains them cheerfully. She enjoys the unreserved friendship and confidence of the people and has much influence over them."

Her work was beginning to bear fruit, but she had not satisfied her soul-longing to start the upriver trek. She could see an improvement in the manners and morals of the peoples with whom she labored. It was a glorious day when the heathen god of the town was vanquished and the chiefs admitted that their laws and customs were not God's laws. Finally, to her delight, the old chieftains made laws against the murder of twins, human sacrifice, the flogging of women by the Egbo runners and other heathen customs.

"One evening I was sitting on the veranda talking to the children," she writes, "when we heard the beating of drums and the singing of men. Taking the twin boys, I rushed out. A crowd of men were standing outside chanting and swaying their bodies. They were proclaiming that all twins and twin-mothers could now live in the town and if anyone murdered the twins or harmed the mothers, he would be hung."

At this glad news the mothers of twins who lived at the

mission laughed and shouted, clapping their hands in delight, saying in sing-song voices while tears coursed down their cheeks, "Thank you! Thank you!"

"It was a glorious day for Calabar. I wept tears of joy. A few days later, the papers were signed and twin-mothers were actually sitting on the platform, a thing unheard of before. The din was terrific, and when I asked the chief to stop the noise, he said:

" 'Ma, how can I stop them women mouths? How can I do it? They be women.' "

Mary gave a graphic description of the clothing the people donned for the occasion; the men draped their bodies in pants without shirts and wore any headgear they could find. Some put on uniforms with gold and silver lace; some wore jeweled hats and caps. Many merely covered their bodies with beadwork and tablecloths trimmed with gold and silver. The Egbo runners were the most gorgeous. "Some wore three-cornered hats with long plumes hanging down. Some had crowns. Some wore masks with animal heads and horns. All were looped around with many skirts and trailed yards of material after them finished with a tuft of feathers at the end."

This enthusiasm waned eventually. Mary found that without the aid of Christ enthroned in the natives' hearts, where custom was pitted against regulations, custom inevitably won. Soon, in the outlying towns and in the remote bush regions, the custom of killing twins was subtly re-established. Patiently Mary labored to establish the true remedy: the Gospel of Christ working in the lives of the transformed natives.

Her passion for work, her zeal and faith were untiring. She was eager to carry the Gospel's redeeming hope to the people in the vilest haunts in town and bush. Often in a canoe she paddled up one of the tributary creeks to districts which no white woman had visited.

Her knowledge of the language, her glowing face and the love that emanated from her soon won the savages and they came to hear with gladness her "Jesus talk." Always she carried medicine for sick bodies as well as Christ's remedy for their sin-sick souls. She found that human ministrations did far more to break down the wall of heathen opposition than her talks given at Sunday meetings. Sometimes as she distributed medicine, the people thronged about her, and with eager ears heard her tell of Jesus' love for them and His death that they might be saved from eternal death and made pure.

Finding that she could not return to the mission compound when night overtook her, she gladly slept in the open with a bundle of rags for covering. These trials she accepted as love burdens; she realized that physical handicaps and hardships meant little in comparison with the grandeur of the soul-triumphs she was able to achieve thereby. Mary's heart was filled with the Master's presence and she was willing to be spent in His service.

One such jaunt took her farther afield than customarily, and the news of her work reached the ears of King Okon, who lived upriver a great distance. Amazed by the stories of the white Ma's love for the bush-blacks, he sent an invitation for her to visit his section. When news reached Old Town, King Eyo Honesty VII, Christianized and letter-writing friend of Mary's mother, decided that this was not a mere visit but a state affair, for which proper preparation must be made. Consequently he sent the royal canoe for her to use in the visit.

"Our Ma," he said proudly, "must not go as an ordinary traveler to this savage land and people, but as a lady and our mother, one whom we greatly respect and love. The canoe is yours to use as long as you wish."

This gracious act filled Mary's eyes with tears of appreciation, and, thanking the tall, dignified African monarch, she told him that the gift would be accepted in the Master's Name. The picturesque canoe was long, slim and painted gaily for the occasion. Bright pennants flew free from its prow, and in the center was a shelter to protect the missionary from the sun. Rice bags were heaped here and there as gifts, and a crew of thirty-three paddlers awaited the white Ma's pleasure.

At six in the evening the canoe still lay quietly on the river bank. Crowds of natives surged back and forth into her house and onto the river, saying good-byes and embracing their white Ma, who had gained their respect, broken their reserve and taught them of Jesus their Saviour.

As night settled, the black crew of thirty-three natives bent to the oars, and, as their torches gleamed in the darkness, the boat shot upstream. Mary was starry-eyed that night and rejoiced that at last she was going on a love mission to a darkened section to which no one had yet brought the Gospel's saving story. She lifted her voice in gratitude to God who had sheltered her in Old Town and who was now to be her refuge in the upriver country.

Her sleep was broken by the gentle hum of the Negro boatmen as their melodious voices improvised songs in her honor with a recurring chorus:

Ma, our beautiful beloved mother, is on board. Ho! Ho! Ho!

She fell asleep to the melody, and the canoe carried her silently through the night. When dawn broke, they had reached Chief Okon's village. A tremendous shout of welcome rang through the African bush, and on disembarking, the missionary was taken to the chief's compound where she was given the master's room, opening into the women's yard. She found no door, but at her request a piece of cotton cloth was hung as a screen to provide privacy. Native etiquette demanded that the chief's wives sit as near as possible, and, fattened according to custom, they perspired freely. The place was rat-infested and overrun by massive lizards and many insects which added to the discomfort of the missionary.

Crowds milled into the yard and pushed aside the harem inmates that they might see for the first time a white woman. For many, seeing was not enough, and they touched her flesh curiously. Some were afraid, and their companions dragged them laughingly into the yard. Confusion reigned throughout the day. When Mary ate, the curious crowds carefully watched her every move.

Mary was not to be discouraged by such antics. She determined to let them eye her body, handle her flesh, even pinch her, that they might take her medicines and listen to her message of Jesus. She cut garments and taught the women the rudiments of sewing. She tried to improve their eating conditions and sanitation. Daily, morning and evening, she faithfully conducted Gospel services.

Always she spoke freely about Christ, the Great Father of all, and His care and love for these His black children who must come to love Him as she did. She taught them of conversion by coming to Jesus, who would forgive their sins. She made the Sunday services impressive by arranging a white tablecloth over a stand. On this she placed her Bible, a hymnbook and if possible a bouquet. She insisted that the compound remain quiet and asked that the attendants be dressed as neatly as possible. Those who came were charmed by her sincerity and listened intently.

So large was the crowd that sometimes her voice barely reached the outside ring of listeners. She told them of Jesus and His power to save them, and when the service was over many came with thanks for the message. Thoughtfully they slipped through the jungle paths, pondering in their hearts the message of truth and hope which Mary had given them. She supported every message with prayer, and trusted that God would bring to fruition the Gospel seed she had planted in their hearts.

She asked the chief for permission to follow the people to their jungle homes, but he would not permit this because the region was "elephant country," to her a new hazard. He told her that the elephant stampedes had been so severe that the people were forced to abandon their gardens and adopt fishing as their means of livelihood.

One morning a great commotion interrupted Mary's devotions, and she rushed out to see the men armed with clubs, swords and all types of jungle weapons fighting a huge boa constrictor which had slithered into the compound. Then she realized the dangers she must face in her tomorrows. In Scotland she had been afraid even of a mouse, but now she must have God-inspired courage to brave boa constrictors, powerful enough to crush the life from her, and elephants so ferocious that they uprooted trees.

Everywhere, even on short jungle trips, the people swarmed about her. Inquisitive eyes searched her face; eager hands sought help and hope. She saw skulls from which the flesh had been bleached, amulets, images and offerings for the gods. The people whispered to her concerning the ravages of witchcraft and poisoning.

One night she saw the people's faces cloud as though a hurricane had swept across them, and found that two of the king's numerous wives, because they had broken a taboo and entered a room where a young boy slept, were to be flogged with a hundred stripes. Mary tried to soften the king's decree.

"Ma, big palaver be proper," he said after listening to her

pleadings for the girls. "And if you say we must not flog, we must listen to you as our guest and mother. But they will say God's Word be no good, if it destroy the power of the law to punish evildoers."

Seeing the logic of the king's words, Mary spoke to the offending girl wives, saying, "You have brought shame by your folly . . . God's Word teaches men to be merciful but it does not countenance or pass over sin. I cannot ask that you be not punished. Ask God to keep you in the future that your conduct may not be a reproach."

The king accepted the good advice and his leading men gave gratified grunts of approval. Then Ma turned swiftly to the gathering, and challenged them:

"You are to blame. Your system of polygamy is a disgrace and a cruel custom. These girls are but sixteen years old and still love fun and frolic. They mean no real harm."

"If the punishment is severe," grunted the old men as she attacked their custom, "neither wife nor slave dare disobey. Old ways are best."

Mary began once more to plead for mercy, and the number of stripes was reduced to ten each. Ordinarily salt would have been rubbed into the wounds, but this was not done. When the beatings were over, she prepared her remedies. She did all in her grasp to alleviate the girls' sufferings, telling them meanwhile of Christ's power to save their souls as she healed their bodies. The girls listened with awe, while the crowd shouted its encouragement to Mary.

Weeks passed, and the time came for the return trip. With great commotion the king and his people bade Mary farewell. Many eyes were filled with tears, and the thunder of their acclaim and invitation to return rose to the heavens, which by this time were darkening with an oncoming storm. The men shoved off the canoe on the homeward voyage, and Mary, resting under a canopy of canvas, gave thanks to her Master for this first experience of jungle life. Her soul rejoiced in the Almighty and His power to save even the most degraded.

Despite the arising storm clouds, she magnified the Lord. When night fell, the downpour of rain drenched both the canoe and its passengers. The rain whipped the raging current into a frenzy, and Mary at last commanded the men to pull for a near-by island. Soon they were under a sheltering tree, and the natives grasped the overlapping branches that they might steady the canoe until the storm passed.

Mary was drenched, and before morning, was shaking with ague and with fever, which, as the hours passed, increased until the rowers feared for her life. Bending their backs to the oars, they pulled for Old Town. Mary suffered a collapse which made imperative a complete rest before she was able again to assume her duties.

In a few months, during October, 1882, a tornado of which she had been warned ripped the roof from her house, and again she was drenched in an endeavor to save her children. Neighboring traders sheltered her and the "bairns," as she called the rescued black children, but the damage had already been done to her weakened body, and she was ordered home for rest and recuperation.

She decided to take Janie, the little twin rescued from the bush, with her on this return trip, as she feared for the tiny girl's life if left without protecting care. Often by false pretenses relatives of twins left at the mission completed the murderous scheme which had been foiled by the missionary. Mary determined that this should never happen to her black Janie, who was like a sister to her. She wanted her to become a happy and useful girl to prove that the twin superstition was unfounded and untrue. Accompanied by her black companion, in April, 1883, the white Ma, still frail and ravaged by fevers, sailed for Dundee, to visit her homeland once more.

CHAPTER 4

THE JUNGLES OF OKOYONG AT LAST

Troublesome days awaited Mary, but from them sprang a deepened faith and a determination to persevere in spite of the difficulties in her path. Her health was soon restored by the home atmosphere and the friendly associations with Mother Slessor, her sisters and Christian friends. She spent much time in the Downfield house and was thrilled by the privilege of telling Mother Slessor about the Christian triumphs she had witnessed in Calabar and the upriver jungles.

Little Janie, her beloved black girl, was carefully taught more about Jesus, and Mary had the joy of seeing her baptized, after her conversion, at the Wishart Church, which the missionary had attended as a child.

During this time she also made many valuable friends, and influenced several to labor in Calabar, among whom were three young ladies, the Misses Hoag, Wright and Peacock, who were to become dearly loved associates. Mary's fame as a missionary caused her to be invited far and near to tell Christian groups of Calabar, and always she took Janie, the little dark girl, with her. Janie was a living witness to the success of the African work, and with her black skin and solemn eyes, she aroused much interest among the young people present in the meetings, who wanted to fondle her and give her presents.

So successful was Miss Slessor in arousing missionary interest through these deputation meetings that the Board decided it would be wise for her to remain longer and visit various churches to promote the Calabarian work. Mary accepted this as the divine will in spite of the fact that her heart was already in Africa where she desired to return. A shy woman, she often found it difficult to address meetings where men were present, and she asked that they be excluded so that she might open her soul more freely to the women and reveal in detail how heathenism had degraded their black sisters.

Having completed her deputation work, Mary was ready to return, when, like a scimitar, trouble cut her life. The health of her sister Janie failed, and it was thought wise to take her to a warmer climate. The family finances made this impossible, so Mary considered the possibility of taking Janie to Africa, thinking the mild climate would be beneficial. She mentioned the subject to the Board, whose members voiced a decided "No," saying that this would be an unwise combination of family problems and missionary activities.

At the suggestion of a friend, Mary took her sister to southern England, where the climate was milder. Writing the Board in 1885, she asked if this action would cancel her mission work. A kind reply came, saying that when the way was clear for Mary to return to beloved Calabar, she would be duly reinstated and sent. The Board graciously offered to continue her salary for several months. Mary, always a sensitive soul, decided that she would not accept the allowance, and the stipend ceased at the end of February.

This left her with a sick sister to care for and no salary. Another tragedy struck when Susan, her oldest sister, died suddenly in Scotland. Added to this was the responsibility of caring for little black Janie. When the sister Janie was better and her mother was in the new home, Mary wrote asking the Board to reinstate her, which they did gladly. Plans were immediately made for her to sail.

Again trouble came, and an illness laid Mother Slessor low. Mary in desperation turned to her only source of comfort and help, and on her knees she agonizingly poured out her soul in prayer to the Heavenly Father for guidance.

Like a message brought by angels the thought came to her: *Why not send for my old friend in Dundee to come and care for Mother?* Immediately the arrangement was made. Now the last barrier between Mary and Africa was removed, and she sailed for her adopted country. The weeks at sea in company with black Janie calmed her nerves and restored her health.

On the journey her prayer had often been, "Lord, permit me to go deeper into the jungles for Thee." This had been her desire since the journey to the land of Chief Okon. She felt that, hidden somewhere in the dense forests, dark and verdant, was the place where she would spend her remaining days in bringing the Gospel to tribes who otherwise would never hear it.

She was notified upon arrival that she had been appointed to Creek Town, the settlement farthest up the river, where she was to be associated with the Rev. and Mrs. Goldie, with whom she had sailed on an earlier trip. As soon as she was settled, Mary entered the battle against heathenism with utter disregard for her own strength, life or health. She cared only for the natives' salvation, and if this meant death for the cause, she was fully prepared to give her all. She lived even more simply than before, since all the money she could save was needed at home. While engaged in this fierce battle with heathenism, she suffered the greatest sorrow of her life when the sad news reached her that Mother Slessor had died.

Mary was despondent, and she cried in her loneliness, "There is no one to write and tell all my stories and troubles and nonsense to. All my life I have been caring and planning and living for them, and I am now left, as it were, stranded and alone."

Yet she was not "stranded" and "alone," for the words of Jesus whispered comfort to her: "Lo, I am with you alway, even unto the end . . ."

She felt, even in this grief, that she was being drawn closer to the Master's side. She gave herself wholly and without stint to His service. All human ties were cut and henceforth she lived only for her Saviour.

"Heaven is now nearer to me," she said in the glory of service, "than Britain, and no one will be anxious about me if I go up country."

Up country was where she wanted to be, but whenever she had mentioned the matter to the Andersons, the Board or her mother, the answer had been: "No . . . not yet." Now her mother was gone, and Mary felt the need of the upriver folk. For fourteen years as a child she had prayed to be sent to Calabar, and this dream through prayer had been fulfilled. She had another dream—the dream of going to Okoyong, a district in the triangle between the Cross and the Calabar Rivers.

The tribesmen, she knew, were cruel, and fought constantly among themselves and with other tribes. They practiced customs more revolting than any accepted by the peoples she had thus far evangelized. Although they were physically superior to the Calabarians, they had fallen deeper into the slough of degradation than they.

Mentally and morally they were inferior to any jungle tribe she had met. They practiced twin-murder, and their belief in witchcraft and sorcery and their use of the poison bean and the ordeal of boiling oil marked them for destruction. They plundered and stole slaves; along the jungle paths were secret watchmen ready to murder anyone who might pass. They hated the people of Calabar, and cut off all contact with them, even defying the British Government's rule. At various times missionaries had tried to break through but always had been compelled to flee for their lives.

This was the land Mary passionately longed to evangelize. She was eager to carry the love of Jesus and the story of His redeeming death to the bushmen. She spoke of it occasionally, though the desire had burned in her heart for years. The field had always been considered too dangerous. Mary was confident that she served a danger-destroying and conquering God, who would open the land to her. When scouting parties were sent out by the Calabarian Christian groups, they were refused protection by the chiefs and turned back empty-handed.

Every man carried a weapon, day and night, and when a missionary asked a native why he did this, he replied, "Indoors or outdoors, talking, eating or sleeping, we must be ready to defend ourselves, for we trust no man."

One day Mary was permitted to accompany a group making an exploration. Coming to the district, she tried to gain permission to remain, but the answer was always "No." When Mary told them they should not kill because of witchcraft, they exclaimed, "Then witchcraft will kill us. What, not kill twins? We will have none of such doings."

Still Mary treasured her dream, and her prayer became stronger and more fervent: "Lord, if this is Thy time, let me go."

She recalled that when she had said good-bye to her mother she had told of going to these tribes, and asked if her mother objected to her going.

"You are my child, given to me by God," said her mother, rejoicing through her tears. "I have given you back to Him. Where He sends you, I would have you go."

These were precious words to the missionary from Dundee. The vision was not to be fulfilled for years, but Mary continued faithfully to labor at Creek Town. Her heart was saddened by the loss of her earthly relatives, the poverty she saw, the heathen customs with which she must cope, but with a prayer on her lips she marched steadily toward the land of Okoyong.

For long periods of time she ate only rice and sauce, that her small available food supply might be sufficient to fill the tiny black mouths for which she was responsible. In addition to Janie, a number of children had come under her sheltering wing. Janie was buoyant as a young deer. She followed Mary the entire day and slipped into bed with her at night.

One day a man came to Mary saying that he was the father of Janie, the forsaken twin. "Come and see her," invited the missionary, but the man refused to see his child. At length the missionary persuaded him that he would not be harmed by looking at the child from a distance, and he assented. Mary seized the large bushman by the arm and dragged him to his little girl, putting his strong black arms around her tiny shoulders. At length he took his daughter on his lap and fondled her. After this he came often to visit his child, and brought her food and gifts.

Other little derelicts came to Mary. She gladly accepted these as gifts from God, and felt she must rear them carefully as young Christians. She sought to teach them in her day school, in the Sunday school, and in her Bible classes and "infant classes." She spoke to the natives about the Master's love and smiled her way into dark hearts in her effort to win them to Christ.

"If I told you what I have seen and known of human sorrow," she wrote a friend at this time, "you would weep till your heart ached."

She saw a blind woman in Creek Town, about whom she wrote:

"She is so poor that she has not one farthing in this

world but what she gets from us, not a creature to do a thing for her, her house all open to rain and ruin, and into which the cows rush at times. But blind Mary is our living, bright, clear light.

"Her voice is set to music, a miracle to the people here, who know only how to groan and grumble. She is ever praising the Lord and her testimony to the Saviour is not a shabby one.

"The other day I heard the chief say that she was the only visible witness among the church members in the town, but he added, 'She is a proper one.' Far advanced in spiritual knowledge and experience, she knows the deep things of God. That old hut is like a heaven here to more than me."

When writing to homeland friends, Mary pleaded, "Pray for us. We need your prayers. Pray in a businesslike fashion, earnestly, definitely, statedly."

She had witnessed the power of prayer, and had proved it often, as she was to do more and more in the future. The days became weeks and the years slipped by as Mary busied herself in the daily round of duties, teaching, visiting, preaching the Gospel, going into the yards where she might come into closer contact with the people. Her vision of going to the Okoyong section did not dim, but burned brighter daily. It was nearer being fulfilled than she dreamed.

In the home office a change had come about in 1881, when it was decided that the women workers of Calabar should be placed under an auxiliary and in May, 1886, this was done. The committee in charge of this work reached a memorable conclusion when they indicated their willingness to open Okoyong to the Gospel, and the Board agreed to the proposal. Thus Mary's ambition was finally to be realized.

With her usual dispatch, once the way was clear, Mary

did not wait for the Board to make the arrangements for settlement in the far-away section, but decided to go herself and attend to the matter. King Eyo Honesty VII offered her the royal canoe, saying, "You may use it for this trip." He had equipped it royally, with a carpet, cushions and a curtain to provide seclusion for the white Ma whom he had learned to love.

Having completed arrangements for the trip into this barbarian country, Mary said her farewells, and the blacks pushed away from shore and headed upstream on a voyage which matched in glory Christian's trek to the Celestial City.

Her mind was filled with forebodings, but when Doubt suggested, "What will happen if the Okoyongs are on the warpath?" Faith shouted, "I must put my trust in God, and not in man." She lay back on the cushions and prayed fervently for protection and guidance. Her meals on the trip were to consist of home-made bread, canned meat and tea, which she brewed on a paraffin stove.

Always a lover of nature, she reveled in the beauty around her. The stream stretched ahead, a pathway of shimmering light, banked by banana and palm trees and plants bright with tropical color. The dark-skinned rowers bent to their task with rhythmic motion, shooting the canoe through the waters toward its destination.

At last they reached the landing beach for the settlement of the chief whom Mary wished to see, and embarked on a four-mile hike through the bush to the village of mud huts called Ekenge. The people gathered to receive the white Ma, crowding about her, and calling her "Mother." They were pleased that she had come alone, thus showing her confidence in them. Chief Edem was at home, fortunately—and sober. He welcomed her ceremoniously, and offered her a hut for the night.

Mary was greatly attracted to his sister, known as Ma
Eme, who in the years to come was to prove one of her
most helpful associates in this wild and untamed country.
The missionary determined to visit the neighboring village
of Ifako, two miles distant, but Edem said that the chief of
the village was not a person for her to meet and at the
time was in a drunken stupor. Mary consented to remain
at Ekenge, where she gathered the people for worship.
They sat around her as she told of God's marvelous, gracious love for them, and of His glorious Son who died that
they might be saved. She described the happiness Jesus
would bring to their village by changing their lives when
they came to Him.

"As I lay on a few dirty sticks laid across and across
and covered with a little dirty corn shells," she wrote to
a friend, "with plenty of rats and insects, three women
and an infant three weeks old alongside, moreover, a dozen
goats and sheep and cows and countless dogs outside, you
don't wonder that I slept little. But I had a comfortable,
quiet night in my own heart."

It was this inward calm which gave her quietness and
peace wherever she might be. She was not affected by
her surroundings, for she was happy in the knowledge
that she had at last reached the land of her desire and
Jesus was with her.

In the morning she was awakened by a shout, and leap-
ing up, she found that two women had been fired at from
the surrounding jungle. The men, grasping their guns and
swords, rushed against the enemy, only to find that the as-
sailants had escaped in the bush and the hunt was abandoned. This made the dauntless missionary compare this
utterly pagan region and people with those with whom she
had worked who had been influenced by civilization and
the transforming power of the Gospel.

Later, when the chief was sober, she went to the Ifako village, where she consulted the headman, who was completely captured by the white Ma's charm and personality, her fearlessness and genuine interest in the welfare of his people. He and Edem granted Mary's request to establish a mission in the region. Each agreed to provide a site for a schoolhouse and a mission building, and these were to be a place of refuge for criminals, for those accused of witchcraft and those to be killed in lieu of the dead. Mary's house was also to be a similar sanctuary.

Thanking them for their kindness, she immediately selected the sites, one at Ekenge and the other at Ifako, a half-hour walk apart. She knew the people were not dependable, and would move to various sections of the region, which would necessitate her moving with them. But this untoward prospect did not deter her. She was willing to hang her hammock under a different tree every night that she might be privileged to give these tribes the Gospel.

Having accomplished her mission, she returned at once to Creek Town that she might make preparations to move permanently to Okoyong, but a sudden downpour turned the river's tide against the paddlers and they had to wait for several hours. Mary was drenched. Watching intently for alligators, she saw a huge snake swim by, followed by a dead body.

She could not sleep, for continually the natives whispered, "Don't shake the canoe or you will wake Ma," or "Don't talk so loud, so Ma can sleep." But when they at last floated freely, she fell into a long sleep, from which she awoke only when Creek Town came into view.

Time passed quickly, for at last she had found the land of her heart's delight, and she did not want to delay her return to the possession God had given.

"Do you think you can have any influence on those savages?" asked a native friend. "They need a gunboat more than a missionary."

Others, feeling that God was with her, were confident that He would make a way for their white Mother, so they assisted willingly with the preparations. They felt that, clad in God's armor she would win. The Christian king, a friend of her departed mother, was on her side, and sent his canoe and paddlers to take her on this long journey. He also afforded a number of bearers who would carry her baggage through the forest from the landing beach.

At last the time of departure came and with good-byes and friendly greetings of affection, the group set out on the day's journey. The missionary's mind was teeming with plans and schemes; tenaciously she clung to the divine promises. There rang in her ears the natives' departing words: "We will pray for you." Said one of her pupils, "I will pray for you, but remember you are courting death."

From the human standpoint that was exactly what she was doing. There had never been a white person who had been permitted to live in this wild region to which she was going. But Mary thought nothing of this. If by her own death she could open Okoyong to Christ's entrance, she was willing to lay down her life.

With her were the five children whom the Lord had enabled her to snatch from death, and also a Mr. Bishop, one of the missionaries who volunteered to make the journey. On a beautiful Saturday evening, August 3, 1888, twelve years after she had first stepped on African soil, this death-defying woman landed among the people whom the world called *impossibles*, but who to Mary were trophies she must win for her Master. Her heart was brave and strong, for God had surcharged it with an overflowing love for the heathen, and whatever the difficulties, she knew she must succeed through Christ, who loved her and gave Himself for her redemption. She was now forty years old, and not a novice.

Could she do less for Him who had died for her? The thought burned in her mind as she undertook this new venture of faith, which was to be a glory-blessed trek through the years.

CHAPTER 5

FACING CRUEL TRIBAL CUSTOMS

"I am going to an unknown tribe up country," Mary wrote a friend. "A fierce, cruel people, and everyone tells me they will kill me. But I do not fear any hurt. Only, to combat their savage customs will require courage and firmness on my part."

Her hope was in Jesus, who had opened the field to her, and she dared to face any problem. Death held no terror, for she felt that until her work was finished, God's protecting hand would overshadow her.

She had accurately analyzed the people and conditions awaiting her. In the twelve years during her first station duties she had acquired fortitude, trust and an utter reliance on God, which was intensely needed to carry her through new emergencies. Mary was to have no helpers. She was alone, and there were no Christian natives to help change the customs. The missionary was the only ray of Christian light in this dense darkness.

She came with prestige, and even to this far-off land of degradation she was known as Ma Slessor, the great white Mother. She was loved, discussed and revered. The Calabarian work had enabled her to understand the character of the natives. The people were undependable, changeable, but, like children, when won they were loyal. Many were their superstitions. Their ignorance was depressing. Mary faced, as she well knew, a battle with heathenism at its worst.

She realized the importance of mastering the language. This would draw the people closer to her.

The night shadows were falling when she landed at the beach, and the native village of Ekenge was four miles inland. The rain poured as she and the five children took the trail, followed by Mr. Bishop and, so she thought, the carriers with the needed baggage.

A queer procession started through the dismal forest. First came an eleven-year-old boy, the oldest child of the group, carrying on his head a box filled with tea, sugar and bread. He was followed by an eight-year-old carrying a teakettle and cooking pots. Straggling behind was a three-year-old with Janie at his heels. The children slipped in the mud, were soaked by the rain and, weary, cried from hunger and fright. The jungle was hidden by the darkness and the strange noises filled them with terror.

In the rear came faithful Mary, bearing in her arms a baby girl and a bundle of supplies. Tears brimmed from the missionary's eyes, but she conquered them and spoke cheerfully to the children. Doggedly the missionary caravan plodded on to the savage region. Mary's faith in God's promises never wavered.

On reaching the village, she found it strangely still. She shouted until two slaves appeared with the sad news that at the next village the chief's mother had died, and the people had gone to Ifako for the burial ceremony. Mary could do nothing but wait for Bishop and the carriers. At last messengers were sent to the chief, telling him of Mary's arrival. Meanwhile the children were fed a simple meal, cooked over an open fire in the drenching rain, and put to bed.

When Mr. Bishop arrived he told the missionary that the carriers would bring nothing until the morrow. They were tired and afraid of the wet jungle trail. Since the next morning was Sunday, she must not permit them to work. Needing food and dry clothing, she sent a boy who had come with Bishop to the canoe with a command that the men must bring the supplies.

Unwilling to ask others to do what she could do herself,
she slipped off her muddy shoes and started through the
terror-filled jungle toward the river. Nightbirds flew
hastily away as she startled them, and the unusual noises
frightened Mary. She was conscience-stricken for having
sent Bishop and the native boy back. Nearing the beach,
she met the returning boy, who carried the message that
the men were on a "sit-down strike" until dawn drove the
hidden dangers from the dark forest.

She did not turn back but pressed on, and, on arriving,
splashed through the water to the canoe in which the men
were sound asleep. Mary soon roused them to action, and
with the slaves Bishop had persuaded to come from the
village, the men and goods were soon on the way to Mary's
Promised Land.

Sunday was cloudy, and the missionary's beginning at
her new station was not encouraging. A few women
dragged themselves from the Ifako debaucheries. When
service time arrived, Mary gathered the people about her,
and on what she later termed the "saddest day of my life,"
she told them the story of Jesus and His redeeming love.
There was little to convince her that her invasion of this
jungle was to be victorious. Thankful that she was in
this land she made a beginning, inauspicious, but nevertheless a beginning.

When Chief Edem returned with his people, he assigned
Mary a room in his women's yard, which reeked with dirt
and squalor. She cleaned the mud and filth in her jungle
abode, and asked that a hole be made in the room for a
window which she had brought with her. She hung a curtain over the door, and with her own hands filled the
cracks and holes in the walls with mud. Later she made
a fenced clearing which she could call her own.

After the people had come thronging back, Mary had

her first experience with the natives' appalling practices and customs, far worse than any she had witnessed. A young boy, on returning from Ifako's orgies, attached himself to Mary and insisted upon helping her as much as possible. The people accused him of deserting their ancient practices. Looking out of her room one day, Mary saw the lad standing near a pot of oil which was being heated, and the people were watching eagerly.

At first she did not grasp the purpose of the boiling oil, but soon Chief Edem appeared, and a man plunged a ladle into the oil. The missionary rushed toward the boy, but arrived too late, for already the burning liquid flooded his hands and arms. The lad stood quivering in agony. Mary could do little, so, with a prayer on her lips, she determined that this custom must cease as soon as possible.

Another custom also demanded attention. The greater the danger, the stronger the evil practice, the more valiantly did the missionary attack it. This new problem seemed to be the worst. Word spread that the White Ma at Ekenge could cure the sick, and a chief, living some eight miles away, requested her to bring her healing potions. When the deputation arrived, Mary considered the situation. If the chief died, according to tribal routine, his wives, free and slave, would be killed that he might have company on the long jaunt into the spirit world. If the tribe decided that his death was due to witchcraft, the poison ordeal would be given to determine the guilty person, and many deaths would ensue.

Mary's heart filled with joy at this opportunity to manifest her belief in her Saviour. Her confidence was in the divine power. When she was ready to go, Chief Edem and his sister, Ma Eme, tried to dissuade her.

"It is a long distance. Deep streams are to be crossed, and it is raining heavily," they asserted, knowing that if the chief died there would be riot and murder and their White Ma would be in grave danger.

Finally Edem assented, for Mary knew she was his guest, and he wanted to treat her with the courtesy due her position. Mary took the matter to the Lord, for she was sure that on the slightest provocation Edem would be engulfed in a tribal war. On her knees she settled the question and was convinced that it was God's will for her to go. Her soul was aglow with a heavenly assurance, and she was confident that her journey would be greatly blessed of God.

The rain poured from the heavens, and before Mary and her guard had gone far, the jungles were a raging torrent. The steaming heat became oppressive, and she seemed to struggle against a wall of wet fire. One by one she cast aside her outer garments as she trudged through the jungle morass. At one little village through which she passed the natives stood in silence as she marched by. She feared the people would scorn her because of her appearance and thus harm the cause of Christ's kingdom.

The effect, however, was the opposite, for the people, knowing why she was making the journey, admired her great courage.

Arriving at the village, she found the people in confusion. Some expected to be murdered when the chief died, and the others were eager for the murders and subsequent rioting. Mary went immediately to the chief and began administering to his needs. Wet to the skin, she accepted with a shudder the dirty rags which were handed to her, as she took off her own clothes to be dried.

She found the chief precariously near death. For days Mary nursed him, and she also trained one of the women to aid her. She lifted high the Cross on which Jesus had died for their sins, and with a heart filled with prayer, a soul which threw all its weight into this fray against heathenism, she accepted the challenge in the Master's Name.

Love and prayer and Christian service won, and the chief recovered, which caused the people to want to learn "book," as they expressed it. They also told Mary they would make peace with Calabar and trade with the Europeans. Faith, pitted against the powers of darkness, had won, and henceforth Mary knew that she could enter the district with the Gospel message. When she had completed her labors in the Master's Name, she told the people that she was going back to Ekenge, but would always be their worker, and would send them a teacher as soon as possible.

At Ekenge she found Edem seriously ill with an abscessed back. The chief at first sought treatment from Mary, but one morning she saw a live fowl fastened upon a stick, and lying about the room were eggs and feathers. On the chief's neck and limbs were witch charms. The witch doctor had his hold upon the sick man.

"Ma, you do not know all the wickedness of the black man's heart," said the chief when she upbraided him for this return to witchcraft. "It has been made known to me that someone is the cause of this sickness. Here are the proofs. All these have been taken from my back."

Ma Slessor looked at the motley collection of shot, egg shells, seed and other articles from compound and jungle. Mary knew what this accusation meant. Men and women were to be chained to yard posts and subjected to the ordeal of poison, boiling oil and other torments. She remonstrated, but Edem, with his wives, chief men and prisoners, was taken to a near-by farm to which Mary was forbidden to come.

Knowing that the prisoners were to be killed, the missionary turned to prayer, and implored God to break the custom. Unceasingly she prayed for victory over this evil.

Anxious days followed, and when Edem recovered in answer
to her prayers, the killing of the prisoners was delayed.
When the chief returned to the village, a wild orgy of feast-
ing, dancing and heathen debauchery—the worst Mary had
witnessed—took place. The only visible answer to her
prayers was the release of those whose death had been
decreed. She wondered, "Am I accomplishing anything
for my Master?"

Soon a new problem presented itself—a savage chief's
arrival, which the missionary interpreted to mean trouble.
As she went about her routine duties, she prayed constantly
that bloodshed and death might be averted. The people
began to drink excessively, and Mary was asked to settle
disputes which arose.

When the final night of the visit came, the men were so
intoxicated that Mary knew it would be impossible to
control the situation. When the chief and his men prepared
to leave, the entire village was in a state of frenzy and
wild excitement. Shots were fired, swords wielded. The
crowd milled madly, and Mary, with a prayer for safety
and a quiet departure, rushed into the melee and hurried
the visitors homeward.

Suddenly they saw the plantain sucker with palm leaves,
nuts and a coconut shell near by, the work of a sorcerer.
The men turned and ran back to the nearest village, which
had placed (so the chief and his followers thought) the
"medicine" in their path. Mary, learning of the confusion,
tried to outdistance the racing men, but in the night they
eluded her and hurried on. Finally by means of a short-
cut, she reached the path ahead of them and planted herself solidly in the way.

She prayed that God would give her grace to stop them
in their mad rush into what would be battle. Mary trem-
bled at her own audacity and cried to the Lord for help.

Daunted by her fearlessness, the savages, wild with drink, stopped, argued and protested, but eventually they yielded to her, as quickened by God's Spirit, and when, under the calmness of the little missionary's self-possession, their anger subsided, they began to retrace their steps. However, when they reached the plantain and the sorcery medicine, they would not pass it. Mary contemptuously picked up the "medicine" and, tossing it into the jungle, dared them to pass the place. They regarded her act with horror; inwardly, however, they admired her bold defiance of this cause of death.

Unfortunately, on returning to their own village, they again drank excessively and fighting broke out in the ensuing orgies. Mary, not to be outdone by this wickedness, took a group of Ekenge men and went to the village, where, with native help, she tied the worst offenders to trees and left them to cool themselves in the breezes of the jungle. However, later she released the men, fearful lest wild animals devour them. On returning home, she picked up the plantain shoot, or sucker, saying, "I will plant it in my own yard and see what witchcraft can do."

The next morning Mary was approached by a runner from the village who said the chief had suffered greatly during the night, and that shot, shells and sticks had been taken from his leg because of the plantain. "Give me the shoot for the chief," said the messenger, but Mary refused. She knew that should the shoot be taken to the chief someone would be killed because of the witchcraft belief. Finally she yielded, at Edem's request, and the plantain was taken to the offended chief.

When the shoot arrived, the chief summoned all the people of the village which was thought to be the source of the sorcery and made them take an oath that they had not bewitched him. In addition he demanded a young man as a hostage. Finally one of their finest black youths was captured and carried off. An attempt by the villagers to rescue him would have meant his instant death. In desperation the natives sent for the friendly white Ma to come and persuade the chief to free the lad.

Mary did not desire further association with this evil chief, but she could not refuse the plea for aid. Placing her trust in God, she faced the wild chief, accused him of his wickedness, and challenged him to free the youth. The black man threw back his head and laughed.

"They murdered me in intention if not in fact," Mary said later in speaking of the incident. "And had God not been with me I would have been killed."

Mary continued to plead for the lad, but without success. In dejection she retraced her steps to Ekenge, realizing that she had failed the people who sought her aid. Feeling ran high among Edem and his men, whom he armed lest battle break out at once. Women crept timidly to Mary's room with the latest developments that she might be informed of events.

Suddenly, without explanation or apology, the young man was set free and returned to his village. Again quiet and peace ruled over the wild district. Mary felt she had endured an ordeal as trying as any suffered by the natives.

Living in the chief's harem yard, she came into close contact with heathen customs at their worst. The experience was helpful, yet horrible. Her eyes were opened to the people's needs, especially those of the downcast women, whose burdens she gladly bore.

"Had I not my Saviour close beside me," she said in speaking of what she experienced, "I would have lost my reason."

Her room was next to that of wild Edem's head wife, and near by were the quarters of his five lesser wives. The yard was surrounded by rooms and accommodations for his other wives, who worked on the farms, for visitors, slaves and the children. Also crowded into the space were cattle, chickens, goats, cats, rats and an army of insects from the jungle. The three boys and two girls Mary brought with her shared her quarters. So crowded was the tiny cubicle that at night she had to bring her belongings outside to provide room for the six to sleep. This, in addition to the constant tropical downpours, made life exceedingly difficult.

Had she not been sustained by the presence of Christ, who filled her heart with hope, she would have lost her mental balance. When the crowded conditions became unbearable she would slip away to a corner of the yard and, under a little bush, commit her ways to the Lord.

In Ma Eme, Edem's sister, she found a true friend. Ma Eme watched over the missionary constantly, prepared her food, and tried to make her comfortable. Mary's opinion of her is expressed thus: "She is a noble lady." As the chief's sister, she was often able to give Mary information in crises. While she never openly professed her faith in Christ's saving power, she was nevertheless Mary's greatest human ally.

One day the missionary asked her about some marks, similar to vaccination scars, on her arm. She replied, "These are the marks of my husband. He bit me," and dismissed the subject as if it were a normal occurrence. Later she told Mary the story of her life.

She was the widow of a prominent chief, and on his death had been forced to undergo the chicken ordeal. All his wives, including Ma Eme, were tried. Each brought a fowl, the head of which was cut off, and the guilt or innocence of the wife was decided by the direction in which the headless fowl fluttered. So great was the strain that

Ma Eme fainted when the witch doctor pronounced her guiltless as the headless bird fluttered madly on the ground.

Mary had a great love for the black children. Often intoxicating drink was given them that they might entertain the elders with their antics. They stole, lied, and did everything in their power to avoid being beaten, branded with fire or otherwise mutilated. Little more than animals, they were treated with less respect than beasts of burden.

Mary labored daily to teach them about Jesus who loved children, and sought to win them before they had become deeply entrenched in heathen ways. The battle was hard, but Mary marched forward with her head held high, for she was obeying the orders of Christ, whom she was bringing to these people who never had heard of Him. Lonesome at times for the companionship of white people, she always found refuge under the wings of the Almighty.

CHAPTER 6

BUILDING FOR GOD IN THE JUNGLES

Chief Edem had promised Mary a house and the villagers had agreed to build it. She wanted to be settled permanently; only then could she change the entire outlook and life of the jungle people through the Gospel message of salvation. Nevertheless, the building of the house was postponed until "tomorrow," which seemed never to come.

Taking matters in her own hands, the aggressive missionary cleared a place in the bush with the aid of her children and those of the natives. She made a game of the work, and when the bush was cleared, she and the children stuck sticks into the ground for the walls and proceeded to thatch the roof with palm leaves. Soon the indolent villagers became interested and offered their help. It was not long until the sticks became two rooms, and the house boasted a fair-sized veranda.

A shed was added, which afforded storage space and additional sleeping quarters if and when necessary. The walls were of interlaced bamboo sticks, beaten until soft, daubed with mud until hard, and then rubbed until smooth. One room was graced with a fireplace of hardened mud and near by was a sideboard and dresser of the same material. Niches were cut into the fireplace and wall for dishes and cooking utensils. Mary polished everything with a native dye, even the mud seat she built near the fireplace. Nor did she forget to make a mud sofa on which to rest in her moments of leisure. It is doubtful if ever a missionary lived in a more cosy and comfortable mud house than Ma Slessor's.

Moving from the chief's yard to her own mud palace was an unforgettable event. Boxes, books, simple furniture, her prized sewing machine, rusted by the dampness, and a little organ, exceedingly useful in church services, were carried ceremoniously into the new home. The entire village watched with interest. Never had their dark eyes seen such a house. To Mary, and to them, it was a haven where she could carry on the work so dear to her heart. Here was seclusion and quiet, even though there were no knives and forks, and though an abundance of insects, and not a few snakes took residence there.

Mary also had plans to build a church and a schoolhouse, which she decided should be built at Ifako, a larger, permanent section. But always the chief was reluctant to fulfill his long-forgotten promise. One morning a messenger arrived from the chief, saying, "My master wants you."

Mary, accustomed to such autocratic commands, went to the village, where she found the chiefs gathered around a cleared piece of ground, on which lay all the essentials for church building: sticks, mud, palm leaves and other materials. The group was eager for Mary's command to build, which was not long in coming. When the building was finished it measured approximately twenty-five by thirty feet. Two rooms were added for Mary should she wish to remain overnight. All were keenly interested in the building, including her letter-writing friend, King Eyo Honesty VII, in Calabar, who had furnished mats for the roof, thousands of which he had brought by canoe to the Ekenge landing. From here free women, of their own volition, and slaves, forced by their owners, carried the mats, and then assisted in plastering the mud walls, making mud seats, and clearing away the debris. One thing Mary insisted upon: cleanliness in and around God's house. The floors were polished and rubbed as smooth as possible. Mary needed a carpenter to make the windows and doors, but there was none. In God's time, however, one was to come.

It was a glad day of victory for Mary when the first services were held in this Okoyong church. She took out of her mission boxes the world's oddest assortment of clothes, and she insisted that the people don them for the occasion. She taught them that when in God's house they must be clean, properly dressed, and must not carry their weapons into the building. She also told the people that slaves and their children could come to the services and were free to attend the classes.

Day classes and Sunday services were organized for the natives, who were eager to learn "book." The light of Christianity soon began to glow upon dark faces in this the most sin-blackened corner of the world. Busy at work for her Master, Mary reveled in plans for enlarging the mission. She could not be content until the two-room house at Ekenge had become the "back house" of the two-story, veranda-surrounded mission house proper.

This expansion program demanded a carpenter to make the windows and doors. Mary could "mud" a house in, but she wanted the new one to be erected properly. Consequently, in March, 1889, she wrote the *Missionary Record* of the denomination concerning her house and the mission, which she spoke of as a "beautiful building but lacking doors and windows as there is no carpenter to do this work." She also expressed a desire to do this properly, for "should I be unable to continue the work, any missionary can come and take it up."

This led the Mission Board to make an appeal for a practical carpenter who was willing to go to Calabar for the needed work. Fortunately, at the time a Mr. Charles Ovens, a member of the Free Church, was in Edinburgh, and was about to sail for America. Seeing the appeal, he immediately decided that this was God's call, since from his boyhood days, he had longed to be a missionary. Consequently, in May of that year he sailed, and on arrival at Duke Town started for Ekenge, taking with him a native helper.

He found Mary at dinner, hatless, shoeless, sitting at the table in the compound, surrounded by her dark-skinned "bairns" and a noisy group of goats and hens. Mary leaped to her feet and greeted the genial Scot joyfully. He was God's answer to her prayer, and she was to depend upon him greatly in the future. His spirit was buoyant, and his cheerful demeanor made him a favorite with all. His Scottish voice rang with the songs of the homeland which blessed Mary and touched the natives, one of whom remarked, "I don't like those songs. They make my heart big and my eyes water."

At once Ovens went to work on Mary's favorite project and the people assisted gladly wherever possible. The eagerness with which the natives helped build the church hall and the mission house caused Mary to realize that they enjoyed helping, and she sought other practical means by which she could enlist their aid.

Intoxication became one of her chief problems at Okoyong, for all the people, even the children, drank excessively. One old man told her, "I have never passed a day in my whole life without drinking," and she felt that she must do something to break the power of drink. She noticed that while the natives were building the house and the church, they took little time for drinking and the orgies which followed.

For some time she had been trying to persuade the chiefs that they should barter with the coast traders, but they merely turned a deaf ear to her appeals. Now she decided to create in them a desire for certain articles by displaying her possessions and pointing out their usefulness in daily living.

The chief, eyeing the doors and windows, grunted his satisfaction. The women enviously fingered the clothes sent from Scotland in mission boxes, and looked longingly at her sewing machine. The clock on her mud mantel caught their fancy. She wrote to the coast towns and tried to persuade the native traders to make an up-country journey with dishes, dress goods, mirrors and other colorful merchandise. Their fear of the native guards, stationed on the paths, caused the traders to refuse the request.

She wrote to good King Eyo, telling him of her problem, and asked him to invite the Okoyong chiefs for a conference. She told him she would induce the chiefs to bring such articles as the jungle afforded for barter.

In due time the invitation arrived, but Mary found it extremely difficult to persuade the chiefs to accept it. She told them of the interesting experiences awaiting them at the coast. The chiefs prepared to go, and collected two canoeloads of plantains, barrels of oil and other jungle products. Many of the natives disappeared in the jungle when they learned that they must leave their weapons at home.

"Ma, you make women of us," pleaded those who remained. "Would a man go among strangers without arms?"

Mary was insistent. She sat down and waited while the beach filled with villagers who wanted to watch the departure of their chiefs. After two hours of arguing and protesting, the men took off their swords and handed their guns to their White Ma. Those who had retreated into the bush reappeared and decided to accompany their companions. As a canoe rowed off, one of the bags shifted and the missionary's quick eye caught the gleam of flashing swords. Deftly seizing them, she threw the implements of war into the river.

King Eyo Honesty VII received the visitors royally, discussed the Gospel with them, told them of its meaning for their lives, and finally took them to his palace where services were held in their honor. The junglemen were delighted with the reception and soon the articles they brought were bartered for goods they were to take home, where another reception awaited them. The following day Mary heard one of the men describing with glowing eloquence the things he had seen and the dignity of the king.

A new world burst upon their gaze when they saw how the Europeans lived. Mary had accomplished her purpose. The men found they had less time and inclination to drink and quarrel. Although the Gospel was going forward and lives were gradually being altered by the power of Mary's righteous influence and teaching, the work of changing the jungle of Okoyong was far from completed.

One day while Ovens was working on the mission house, Mary heard a weird sound which came from the near-by jungle. She listened intently for a moment, and then leaped to her feet. "Something is wrong in the bush!" she exclaimed. One of her boys soon returned with the news that a young man had been found nearly dead, and Mary, equipped with medicine, hastened to the scene. Looking into the young man's face, she said, "It is Etim, the son of our chief, Edem. He is to be married and is building his house. A tree slipped and struck him. He is paralyzed and that means serious trouble. It will be considered the result of witchcraft."

A carry-all was hastily constructed, and the lad was taken to his mother's home at Ekenge. For two weeks the missionary faithfully nursed him day and night, pouring her strength, her knowledge of medicine, and her prayers into the work of mercy. Sunday morning Mary could see that the end was near. She left his side for a short time but, upon hearing him groan, rushed to him.

The natives were blowing smoke into the young man's nostrils and rubbing pepper into his eyes while his uncle, Ekponyong, shouted into his ears. The young man died almost instantly, and the natives shouted, "Sorcerers have killed him and they must die! Bring the witch doctor at once!"

Men and women disappeared rapidly, and soon only Mary and the workers were left. When the witch doctor came, he declared that the people of a certain village were to blame. Armed men were sent to sack the settlement and seize the inhabitants, but the chief, Akpo, had heard the news, and his people had fled into the bush, except for a few who remained and were captured. Their houses were burned, and the captives were taken to Ekenge.

Mary was certain that the captives would be subjected to the ordeal of the poison bean. A small brown bean which grew in the bush was crushed, put into water, and then given to the suspect as a test of his innocence or guilt. The bean was poisonous, and those who drank the water died. Even though death was inevitable, the natives believed that justice had been done. If the captives had been innocent, argued the tribesmen, they would have lived. The fact that they died proved them guilty.

The missionary quickly devised a plan by which to honor the dead young man. She wrapped the lad's body in silk, and dressed him in the finest suit available. Then she wound a silk turban around his head and completed his attire with a high black and scarlet hat trimmed with brilliant feathers.

Thus bedecked, the corpse was carried into the yard and seated in a large chair under an umbrella. In the young man's hands were the whip and silver-headed stick which indicated his position as a chief's son. He was also given a mirror in which he could behold his glory. On a near-by table were his treasures, including skulls he had taken in war.

When the people were admitted to the yard, they shouted, danced with delight, and called for liquor, which increased their frenzy. As the natives opened case after case of whisky, the orgies grew wilder. The dusky savage faces, the dense jungle and the deepening gloom of night, relieved by the wild glare of torches, added to the weirdness of the scene.

Mary and Mr. Ovens, fearing lest they be murdered, took turns watching the prisoners. Returning to her hut, Mary saw several poison beans on the pounding stone. Cold with fear, the missionary, until now fearless amid jungle dangers, fell on her knees and submitted the problem to the Lord. With calm assurance she went to Edem and his brother, Ekponyong, and told them firmly that the poison ordeal must be forbidden.

Mary, realizing that her arguments were futile, went to the gate of the compound, where the prisoners were kept, and seated herself, fully determined not to move nor let anyone reach the victims. The chiefs became enraged and the mob howled violently as the natives brandished guns and swords.

"Raise our master from the dead," they shouted, "and we will free the prisoners!"

Steadfastly the missionary kept her vigil. Meanwhile she scribbled a request for help, which she sent to Duke Town secretly. Mary suddenly detected a mysterious movement in the frenzied crowd. A man pushed through the throng, brushed her aside, placed the chains on a woman and, commanding her to take her place in front of the corpse, ordered her to drink the poison.

The other victims pleaded with Mary. "Do not go and leave us," they begged as the frightened woman prepared to drink the poison.

Praying for God's help in this time of need, Mary approached the victim. The woman had already raised the glass containing the poison. Mary whispered, "Run," as she seized the woman's hand. Before the crowd discovered what had taken place, the missionary and the condemned native were deep in the jungle. They sought refuge in Mary's hut, which was a sanctuary for condemned criminals. Ovens took the woman into the compound, and Mary, thanking God for this miraculous escape, returned with the remaining prisoners.

The struggle was resumed, and the chiefs declared that an innocent person would not die if he drank the poison. Mary and Ovens attempted to appease the irate chief by offering to release some of the prisoners, and when Edem asked that a coffin be made for his son, Ovens complied, though with some reluctance. All except three of the prisoners were released. Two were related to the dead boy's mother and were thus involved in the tragedy, and the other was a relative of Chief Akpo, the leader of the suspected village.

"We have done more for you than we have done before, and we will do nothing else," said Edem when Mary asked that these three prisoners also be liberated.

Visitors from other villages arrived, and news came that Egbo runners were on their way. Mary was advised to leave if she valued her life. Edem, violently angry with Mary, threatened to destroy the mission house. Ma Eme intervened and begged her brother to chain the one prisoner who remained in the yard (the others had been led away to the missionary's veranda). Mary approved of the idea, and to her delight, Edem yielded. This would give the prisoner an opportunity for a fair hearing.

Meanwhile two missionaries arrived from Duke Town in response to Mary's summons. Their presence gave prestige to the dead and compensated for the lack of human sacrifice. They presented a magic-lantern exhibition which delighted the savage people and calmed the riot. Chief Edem continued to insist, however, that the remaining women be given the poison, and he ignored Mary's pleading. When the funeral occurred, however, a cow was killed and placed in the coffin—not the men and women who were suspected of witchcraft.

Mary had achieved one of the greatest victories of her career, but more trouble was ahead. The Egbo runners threw the village into pandemonium. Panic-stricken, the women and children, who were slaves, hurried to Mary's house for protection. The house was filled to capacity with these refugees, who stayed with Mary until the runners left.

After several weeks, the chained prisoner in Mary's hut was released on the condition that if Chief Akpo was caught, he would take the poison. Mary, weary from the strain of the ordeal, was grateful that God had enabled her to win the victory. She learned that this was the first time in the history of Okoyong that a chief had been buried without human sacrifice. Her fame spread rapidly, and the people of the jungle and bush considered this lone White Ma superhuman.

However, the matter was not settled, for soon the young man's uncle, who lived in a neighboring village, was accused of having killed the boy, and he demanded the privilege of undergoing the poison-bean ordeal with the other chiefs, including Edem, the boy's father. When Mary heard of the plan, she rushed to the village and stole the bag of poison beans while the men argued and brandished swords and guns. Later the chief accosted her and demanded the beans, but Mary remained calm and refused to relinquish them.

Akpo, the chief of the accused village, remained a fugitive from justice, and Mary pleaded with Edem that he be forgiven and permitted to return home. Finally God softened the warrior's stony heart, and he agreed to Mary's plan.

"You may tell him," he said, "that all thought of vengeance is gone from my heart. If he wishes to return to his own village he can do so, or he can go anywhere in Okoyong in safety."

Forgiveness was unheard of in the jungles, and Akpo remained skeptical until Mary persuaded him that the chief's forgiveness was genuine. When Akpo returned to his village, he found that the houses had been burned and the cattle stolen, but the familiar scenes of home were still there, and, kneeling gratefully at Mary's feet, the chief promised that he and his house would never oppose her wishes. This was a promise to which he remained true, despite the fact that other chiefs often disputed with Mary and threatened to do bodily harm to the missionary.

Chief Edem was generous to Akpo and his people. He built houses for them and helped to restore their former prosperity. The old chief came to Mary, and, kneeling, thanked her for her courage and perseverance in preventing human sacrifice at the time of his son's death.

"Your ways are better than ours," he admitted. "We are all weary of the old customs."

Secretly the people came and told Mary how grateful they were for the changes she was effecting. They acknowledged the harmfulness and evil of their excessive drinking, and expressed gratitude for the security which Mary had made possible.

Mary's path through the jungle had been difficult, but a beckoning gleam of hope shone in the distance. Never had she refused a call for help, no matter how tangled the dense jungle foliage, dark the night, or heavy the tropical downpour. Never had she left a scene of death or danger until she had done her utmost. Mary was a faithful witness to the saving Gospel she preached.

"She was at their beck and call day and night," testified Mr. Ovens. "She taught in the schools, preached in the church, and washed the wee bairns herself. She nursed the most loathsome diseases when others refused to do so."

"My one great consolation," Mary said concerning those trying days, "was prayer. I did not use to believe the story of Daniel in the lions' den until I had to take some of those awful marches through the jungle. Then I knew it was true. Many times I walked alone, praying, 'O God of Daniel, shut their mouths!' and He did."

Finally fever seized her body and Mary, weak and worn, was forced to prepare for a furlough. As soon as a worker was found to take her place, she engaged steamer passage and prepared for the journey home. Miss Dunlop, the new worker, arrived on the scene just as Mary was preparing to leave. A great crowd had gathered. Suddenly a runner exclaimed, "Come, White Ma, a young man has been shot in the hand and he wants your medicine!"

In spite of friendly protests and the knowledge that she was going to a warlike tribe, Mary prepared for the trip. The journey was difficult and when she arrived, it was already night. The people sat silently in the darkness, bemoaning the accident. Before morning the chief said, "We must avenge this terrible thing," and his men went into the jungle determined to avenge the wrong done to one of their tribesmen.

Weak though she was, Mary overtook them at an enemy village as they were preparing to attack. Earnestly she told them of the terrible evil they were about to commit. A silence followed her words, as she prayed that God might prevent the impending carnage. An old man stepped from the crowd of warriors and, kneeling before her, said, "Ma, we thank you for coming. We admit we wounded the chief of these who have come against us. But it was one man who did it. The whole village is not at fault. Please make peace."

Mary suddenly realized that the old man was speaking of a man whom she had helped when she first came to Okoyong. A long discussion followed. Occasionally the excitement was intense, but ultimately Mary and her God won the victory. Peace was assured when the native promised that there would be no fighting while she was on her furlough, a vow which was kept.

Exhausted, Mary tramped back to Ekenge, where she learned that her baggage was already on its way to the coast and that an escort was waiting to take her to Duke Town. She had spent only three years in Okoyong, but already she could see a subtle change in the heathen minds. In later years she was to witness the glorious transformation which only the Gospel can produce.

CHAPTER 7

THE DREAM THAT DID NOT COME TRUE

Mary arrived in England at the beginning of the year 1891. She had with her little black Janie, who was a lovable companion and a joy to the White Ma. Eager to see those who had been with her mother and sister in their last illnesses, she went immediately to the south of England, where she took a small house and rested until autumn. The bracing air, sweeping in from the sea, and release from the intense labors of Okoyong soon restored her strength.

People were eager to hear of her work, and reluctantly she began to speak in the churches. "It is a trial to speak," she said of these experiences, "but He has asked me to do it and it is an honor to be allowed to testify for Him. And I wish to do it cheerfully."

Often her listeners were disappointed when she delivered an evangelical message which told little of her African work, but when she spoke of Ekenge, the jungle beauty, the savage tribes and Christ's conquering power, her hearers sat entranced. Mary's messages aroused missionary enthusiasm, and committees were organized which sent many boxes to the foreign field.

In September the mission board was surprised to receive a letter from her saying that she was engaged to a twenty-five-year-old mission teacher at Duke Town, Charles Morrison. Although Mary was forty-three at the time, the difference in their ages seemed of little consequence to her. Morrison was a genial Scotsman, a man of high ideals, and well trained. Despite Mary's age she was youthful in temperament, buoyant in spirit and had a keen sense of humor. Before her furlough she told the board of her engagement.

Mary praised her fiancé and assured the board that he

would be a great help in her jungle work. At Okoyong, Morrison had asked Mary if, should the board veto his going to the jungle with her, she would return to Duke Town with him, but she insisted emphatically that her work was in the jungles where no laborers had planted the Gospel seed.

"It is out of the question," she wrote to a friend concerning her departure from Okoyong. "I would never take the idea into consideration. I could not leave my work for such a reason. To leave a field like Okoyong without a worker and go to one with ten or a dozen workers, where the people had the Bible and plenty of privileges—it is absurd. If God does not send him up here, then he must do his work and I must do mine where we have been placed."

She left the matter in God's hands, and was willing to abide by the board's decision. "I lay it all in God's hands and will take from Him what He sees best for His work in Okoyong. My life was laid on the altar for that people long ago, and I would not take one jot or tittle of it back. If it be for His glory and the advantage of His cause there to let another join in it, I will be grateful. If not, I will try to be grateful, as He knows best."

The board disapproved of the marriage and Mary's dream of having someone share her labors did not come true. When the answer came, Mary said, "What the Lord ordains is right." What she suffered no one was to know. The missionary longed for companionship, but, having consecrated her life to God, she was convinced that He must be her first love.

Morrison, however, was broken by the disappointment, and his health soon failed. He was forced to return home, and later went to America, where he died. After Mary's death, two books were found among her treasured keep-

sakes. Her initials and Morrison's appeared in one, and
the other contained their signatures. This loss was among
the many sacrifices Mary made when she offered her life
upon God's altar.

Somewhat disturbed by the broken courtship, Mary continued her speaking engagements until she was stricken
with influenza and bronchitis, which temporarily ended her
public appearances. However, she found time and strength
to write a series of articles for the *Missionary Record*. In
these she pleaded Calabar's cause and maintained that the
Gospel must be preached to the people in that region and
that the natives must be taught self-sustaining trades. The
missionary pointed out that when they were engaged in
trades which they could easily learn, their standard of
living improved.

"Let the science of the evangelization of the nations," she
wrote, "occupy the attention of our sermons, our congregations, our conferences and our church literature, and
we will soon have more workers, more wealth, more life,
as well as new methods."

Mary felt that the task was too great for one missionary
to undertake successfully, but required the attention of
several. Her appeal aroused wide interest. The conserva-
tive Scots viewed the innovation with concern. They talked
to other missionaries and even wrote to the Calabarian
workers to discover their opinion concerning the sending of
industrial and occupational aides to the foreign fields. A
direct result of this enthusiasm was the Hope Waddell
Training Institute, which accomplished much for the evangelization of the west coast of Africa.

Mary's health did not improve, and consequently she and
Janie were forced to spend time at Devon. "Parents alter
things for the children, and God does the same for us," she
said, and accepted poor health as His desire for her. How-

ever, by February, 1892, she was ready to sail for Calabar. Her eventful furlough had ended forever her dream of companionship. She was to find companionship and sympathetic understanding only among the dark people with whom she labored and the Master who sustained her. Henceforth her Heavenly Father was to become increasingly dear.

Returning to Okoyong, she entered again the routine of native life. Her years of self-sacrifice were apparent in the large and attractive mission house, the outbuildings for visitors, and the churches and schoolhouses in many communities. A houseboat had been given her for river travel. She valued these evidences of progress, but more important to her was the fact that heathen customs were gradually being destroyed through the Gospel's power to transform lives.

Throughout the jungle the work of God went forward, and even in outlying districts, which Mary seldom visited, the influence of Christ was felt. The natives were gradually abandoning their heathen customs.

Mary had many friends among the natives, not a few of whom were chiefs, and none were more loyal than Ma Eme. A deep friendship existed between the missionary and this black woman. Often when the chief's sister heard of trouble she sent a messenger to bring Mary a medicine bottle. This meant, "Be ready for trouble." Each night for a month Mary slept fully clothed while she awaited the familiar cry, "Run, Ma, run." Her uncanny knowledge of the warring chiefs' plans led some of them to regard her with awe. They could not outwit her, for she seemed to know their secret plans.

When she was unable to reach the danger scene in time, she scrawled important-looking characters and words on a large sheet of paper, sealed it with red sealing wax, and sent it by swift runner to the chiefs who were intent on trouble. They could not read the message, but since it came from the White Ma, they considered it of great importance. Quizzically they asked, "What can it mean?" While they were trying to solve the mystery, Mary arrived and settled the difficulty.

At other times, when trouble arose, Mary hastened to the scene, put up a large colored umbrella and, seating herself under it, knitted for hours. The assembled chiefs, dressed garishly in costumes from the mission boxes, gathered around, surrounded by their armed warriors, who were ready at a moment's notice to fly at each other's throats. Outwardly calm but inwardly frightened by the armed warriors, Mary sat knitting quietly while the discussion was held.

While the chiefs stated their arguments, she listened attentively. Hours passed as the natives argued. When Mary grew weary, she called a chief forward to summarize the case, and then she gave the verdict. The warriors lifted their voices in excitement, but when the verdict was given, it was sealed by a native oath, and the hungry and exhausted missionary tramped wearily to the mission house, happy that the fire of a smoldering battle had been quenched without the loss of life.

During this time another honor came to Mary. She was appointed vice-consul for the British Government among the Okoyong natives. Changes were rapidly taking place in the government as a result of the altered customs of the people. In 1889 the leading chiefs agreed to the establishment of the Niger Coast Protectorate, and two years later Sir Claude MacDonald was appointed consul. However, he found that Okoyong was completely under the power of Mary's personality, and he gave her the honor of serving under him.

Mary knew her jungle people would not allow an outsider to introduce new laws and settle native disputes arbitrarily. She therefore sought authority to organize and direct a native court, which was to be entirely under her jurisdiction. Acting as consular agent, she participated in all tribal public affairs. When legal difficulties arose she traveled to the outlying districts where she tried the culprits.

This brought the natives to Mary for advice regarding their customs and the new laws. Motivated by love for their spiritual welfare, she ruled with justice and did much to establish laws for the protection of the poor and helpless. Government authorities were astounded by her influence over the bush people. Her wit delighted them, and they admired her skill in solving difficulties.

"What sort of woman I expected to see I hardly know," wrote an official. "Certainly not what I did. A little lady with a lace shawl over her head and shoulders—swaying herself in a rocking chair and crooning to a black baby in her arms. Her welcome was everything kind and cordial. I had had a long march; it was an appallingly hot day, and she insisted on complete rest before we proceeded to the business of court. It was held just below her house. Her compound was full of litigants, witnesses and onlookers, and it was impressive to see how deep was the respect with which she was treated. She was again in her rocking chair, surrounded by ladies and babies and holding another infant in her arms."

Mary settled all difficulties justly. Those were trying times for her, for she realized that her missionary endeavors could be hindered by the decisions which she made.

"I suppose that a pluckier woman has rarely existed," wrote another government official. "Her lifework she has carried out with immeasurable courage and capacity.

. . . Shrewd, quick-witted, sympathetic, she would with wonderful patience hear all sides equally. Her judgment was prompt, sometimes severe, but always just."

Officials rarely came into the neighborhood without seeing her. One said facetiously, "They were given over to Mariology." They discussed their work and ambitions with her as with a mother or a sister. Many times when officials were transferred to other districts, they wrote her affectionate and grateful letters, a further evidence of her glowing Christian personality. She was able to understand and influence her fellow countrymen as well as the jungle people.

This official friendliness was helpful, for Mary was given permission to use government conveniences on roads and rivers. Workmen were sent to repair her house, and they brought her many gifts. Officials worried about her health, for she ignored the tropical precautions against diseases common to the region. She went hatless, although the Europeans thought it necessary to don helmets whenever they were in the sun; she refused to use mosquito netting. Mary, her friends and officials at Duke Town and elsewhere exchanged letters regarding these precautions.

"Do take quinine and sleep under a net and drink filtered water," was a warning she received frequently. "We know why you will not wear a hat," said another, chiding her. "You want to show off that pretty hair of yours. Fancy a great missionary like you being so vain!"

These pleadings did little to alter Mary's mode of living. She lived the native life as she had adopted it from the start, at first from necessity to reduce expenses so that she might have money to send home, and later because this mode of living suited her work. She ate native foods and her meals were irregular. It was not an uncommon sight to see her going barefoot through the jungles, even though snakes, insects of many kinds and poisonous plants infested the regions through which she traveled. Her clothing was simple and she was constantly ready to answer a call for help.

She viewed no task as menial. To her, patching a roof and whitewashing the mud plaster were tasks as sacred as teaching the children how to read or conducting a church service. Her work was for Christ and to save souls. Her mission was to transform lives by the living Gospel, and there was no division of her labors into "secular" and "sacred" duties. All her tasks were sacred and part of the work to which the Master had called her.

"Consecrated, affectionate women who are not afraid of work"—these were the workers whom she considered to be qualified. "Women who can nurse a baby or teach a child to wash and comb as well as read and write. Women who can tactfully smooth over a roughness and for Christ's sake bear a snub, and take any place that may open. Women who can take everything to Jesus and there get strength to smile and persevere and pull under all circumstances. Up in a station like mine, they need to teach the first principles of everything and to help in time of trouble in the home or in the town palaver."

In her notes made from time to time, Mary never used the pronoun *I* but always used the term *we*, realizing that she was a co-worker with the Almighty.

"We do not attempt to give in numbers those who are nominally Christian. All the children within reach are sent to the school without stipulation. No ordained minister has ever been resident or available for more than a short visit, so no observance of the ordinance of baptism or of the Lord's Supper has been held. Nor have we the usual definite offers of persons as candidates for church membership. We have just kept on sowing the seed of the Word.

"Of results affecting the condition and conduct of our people it is generally more easy to speak. Raiding, plundering and the stealing of slaves have almost entirely ceased. It would be impossible, apart from a belief in God's particular and personal providence in answer to prayer, to account for the ready obedience and submission to our judgment which was accorded us.

"No tribe formerly was so feared because of their utter disregard for human life. But human life is now safe. No chief ever died without the sacrifice of many lives, but the custom has now ceased. A native speaking of the death of a prominent chief at which no life was taken said, 'Ma, you white people are God Almighty. No other power could have done this.'

"In regard to infanticide and twin-murder, there has dawned on them the fact that life is worth saving, even at the risk of one's own. Though chiefs and subjects less than two years ago refused to hear of the saving of twins, we already have their promise and the first installment of their fidelity to this promise."

The Gospel was thoroughly at work, leavening the tribesmen and changing their lives. Drinking, among the women especially, decreased. Roving bands of disreputable women who formerly visited Mary disappeared. "In our neighborhood it is a rare thing," the missionary wrote, "to see an intoxicated woman even on feast days and at funerals."

The people showed an eagerness for education, which caused Mary to call for teachers. Schoolteaching was difficult. The population was scattered, the family quarrels severe, and the fear of evil spirits, thought to live in the forests, caused the children to dread the journeys to school. Added to these handicaps were wild animals which roamed the jungles. Furthermore, the girls were withdrawn from school to be fattened for their husbands, and the boys were irregular in attendance because of tribal customs.

"There have been difficulties on our side, too," the missionary wrote. "The distances consume time and strength, the multifarious claims made on the mission house, the household itself which is usually a large one, having in addition to servants those who are training for future usefulness and rescued victims of heathen practices. The dispensary calls for strength. Then one must be ever ready to hear complaints and to shelter the runaway slave wife or victim of some superstition . . .

"Add to this, housekeeping cares with no butcher, baker, water, gas, coal or laundry supplies. After all this is seen to day by day, you may judge where is time and strength for teaching and evangelistic work."

Mary wrote glowing accounts of changes which God had wrought among the natives. This work required patience, iron nerves and Christlike love. As time passed, improvement continued, and the tribesmen showed a growing interest in Mary's work. She received many gifts. The little steamer, which the natives called *Smoking Canoe,* delighted Mary's heart. This gift was made possible by the contributions of children in her homeland. Success crowned her labors, and she could no longer be content to rest at ease in her Okoyong Zion.

Mary had a burning zeal to go forward. Now that comparative peace and semicivilized conditions prevailed in the jungles to which she had given her life and love, she longed to move to a new field where Gospel seed had not yet been sown.

CHAPTER 8

THE RICH FRUITAGE OF THE OKOYONG LABORS

When Mary had come to Ekenge, she had attacked a wholly uncivilized and barbarous tribe with the Gospel's power and had won. The venture she contemplated was not to be so drastic as this had been. Many of the tribesmen had shifted to various sections in the vicinity, leaving Ekenge sparsely populated. They had discovered that crops grew better in the virgin soils which for centuries had not been used, and consequently they moved their homes. The missionary desired to move with them, that she might not only retain what she had gained, but reach new tribes as well.

Many of her old comrades had gone to Akpap, south of Ekenge and farther inland, which brought her nearer the Cross River, where a native market had been established. This trading center brought heathen to the settlement.

The mission board objected to the move, since it would necessitate a new building project and, furthermore, the nearest landing place was Ikunetu, six miles from Akpap. The intervening forests between the town and the river were wild, difficult to traverse, and more inaccessible than the old location. After much discussion the board granted her wishes and built a mission house at the settlement and a boathouse for her new steamer.

Mary, eager to start her new work, did not wait for the house to be built, but in 1896 constructed a two-room native shed in which she established her headquarters. The hut was not so habitable as her first Ekenge home, but this did not trouble Mary, for her primary concern was to bring the Gospel to the heathen. Prayer and faith compensated for the lack of home comforts.

The work was much the same as that which she had been doing. Chiefs came with their tribal difficulties and the people brought their domestic problems. Visitors from the jungle and bush were numerous. Faithfully she taught classes and conducted her Sunday services. Added to her troubles was a smallpox epidemic. Hour after hour, far into the night, day after day, Mary vaccinated the natives, and when her supply of vaccine was exhausted, she inoculated healthy persons with blood from the arms of those who had received the serum.

The plague was especially serious at Ekenge, which caused Mary to return and convert her former home into a hospital. The sufferers filled it to overflowing, and Mary was forced to serve as doctor, nurse and undertaker. Many of her close friends died, among whom was Chief Ekponyong, and when Edem, the chief of Ekenge, was stricken by the plague, the weary missionary did all in her power to save the old heathen's life. Her constant vigil at his bedside was in vain, for one night, in the jungle gloom, he died.

Mary was alone, and with the courage of a Christian soldier she made the coffin, placed the chief's battle-scarred body in it, and dragged the box to the grave she had dug. She conducted a simple Christian ceremony and prayed as his body was laid away that her words might reach receptive hearts. Exhausted, she trudged back to Akpap.

Fortunately, Mr. Ovens and another missionary arrived from the coast at this time, and when they reached Mary's hut, they found it strangely silent. "Something is wrong," said Mr. Ovens. Knocking loudly on the rude door, they were finally able to arouse Mary and when she told them of the scourge, they were unable to believe that one woman had stemmed the tide of sickness.

A few days later the two men traveled through the for-

est to Ekenge, where they found the mission house filled
with dead bodies. These they buried. Henceforth the
building was never used for human habitation.

Abandoned huts filled with corpses and jungle paths
choked with dead black bodies—these Mary saw, and her
heart was broken, but she kept doggedly at her work.

"Four at my feet listening," she wrote to a friend shortly
after the crisis had passed, and she was back at her tasks.
"Five boys outside getting a reading lesson from Janie. A
man lying on the ground who has run away from his
master and is taking refuge until I get him forgiven. An
old chief with a girl who has a bad ulcer. A woman beg-
ging for my intervention with her husband. A nice girl
with heavy anklets from knee to ankle with pieces of cloth
wrapped around to prevent the skin from being cut. Three
for vaccination."

Day after day these familiar scenes were re-enacted.
Every evening a service was conducted. Mary sat on the
mud floor in one of the shed rooms, and in front of her,
in a half-circle, were the household children. Behind them
were the baskets containing the twin babies she had re-
cently rescued. The light from a small lamp flickered on
intent, black faces. Mary read slowly from the Bible, gave
a brief message from God's Word, and prayed. Then she
sang a song in the native tongue. The tune was a Scottish
melody, and a tambourine provided accompaniment.

Should a listener's attention wander, the missionary
leaned forward and tapped the offender's head with the
tambourine. As Mary sang the beloved Scotch airs, she
remembered home and the loved ones who had entered
eternal life.

The epidemic sapped Mary's strength, and she became
weak and ill. Her furlough was long overdue, and the
Calabar Committee decided that even though no one could

be found to take her place, she should return to her home. Mr. Ovens, the ever-ready carpenter, was building the Akpap mission house at the time, and was appointed to continue the White Ma's work until someone could be found for the task. Consequently, in 1898, the missionary made plans to return home.

The care of her many black children was a serious problem. She did not wish them to return to heathen ways and modes of living, nor did she feel free to ask the other mission workers to assume their care, but eventually they were assigned to various homes, and Mary took her "family" with her. This consisted of Janie, now a young woman of sixteen, Mary, who was five, and two younger children, Alice, three, and Maggie, who was less than a year and a half.

Mary also faced the problem of clothing the family, for the rags the children wore in the bush were not the proper attire for a long and memorable journey to Scotland. Mary's faith was strong, and she brought her problem to the Master, who had many times supplied her needs. God's hand was not shortened in this time of need, and He furnished clothing for her children.

Confident that her Heavenly Father would provide the necessary clothing, Mary went to Duke Town. When she arrived she found that a missionary box containing the needed garments had just arrived. Worn and exhausted, she rejoiced in the Lord, whose eye was ever upon His righteous worker. The ocean voyage was uneventful, even though her brood aroused considerable interest on the liner, and when they arrived in the homeland, the black children were the objects of curiosity.

Mary was enthusiastically welcomed by her Christian friends, and soon found a comfortable little home at Bowden, St. Boswell's. When she had recuperated, speaking engagements were arranged, for her work during the years since she first landed in Calabar had created widespread interest. Mary again found it trying to address congregations, for during many years she had substituted the native African tongue for her mother speech. When she spoke, however, the Holy Spirit touched her faltering tongue, and she delivered a message which gripped her hearers. When Mary described the people and the country from which she had come, her impassioned love made her words unforgettable.

"It is characterized by a simple diction," said a minister in describing her addresses, "a tearful sympathy, a restrained passion and a pleading love for her people, which made it difficult to listen to her without deep emotion."

Mary was a gentle woman, below average height. Her complexion resembled sun-weathered parchment; her hair was short and had turned from red to deep brown. Her voice rang musically as she opened her heart and told the congregations of Christ's conquering power which she had witnessed in Calabar and Okoyong. Not once did she boast of her achievements.

"The other missionaries at Calabar," Mary declared, "work as hard, if not harder, than I do." She pleaded for more workers and often hinted that she would like to go inland again and "make a home among the cannibals." After the restoration of her health she was able to devote herself relentlessly to speaking engagements. During the latter part of 1898 she again turned her face southward, and late in the year she boarded a steamer for Calabar. Mary spent a happy Christmas aboard the ship.

With renewed vigor she resumed her work—teaching, healing the sick, visiting in the bush, preaching to the people. Strangers came to the Akpap house with their troubles, and often a native in the dense jungle would say he knew about Jesus "because the White Ma told me about Him."

During this period Mary had the joy of seeing six of the free-born boys become Christians. These young men she trained and sent to the neighboring villages as Gospel workers. She had hoped for more converts but was grateful that God had given her these. Her fame spread to such an extent that bushmen traveled hundreds of miles to see the White Mother, who told them about Jesus. Many were the times she rushed into the bush to settle a tribal quarrel. Mary eagerly used every opportunity to preach the Gospel to heathen who had never heard it.

The stories which the visiting people told about their lands and the inland tribes aroused Mary's desire to explore, and often in the mission launch or canoe she journeyed to distant regions. On one such journey the canoe was attacked by a hippopotamus, and Mary thought her end had come. Bravely she fought the animal off by using metal cooking utensils as weapons.

In 1900, while her work was progressing steadily, changes were taking place in the government. The country was opening to trade, and the vast region, originally one protectorate, became two: Northern and Southern Nigeria. In Southern Nigeria, a wild region, the government had been unable to conquer the Aros, a powerful tribe which ruled there. These were an arrogant people, similar to the tribes of Okoyong when Mary began to labor among them. They practiced raiding, made war on peaceful tribes, engaged in devil worship, and offered human sacrifices.

Often they practiced cannibalism, and the government determined to stop their evil deeds. Accordingly, a small military expedition was sent inland in an effort to make them obey. This grieved Mary, for she knew that the Gospel alone would change the black men's hearts. She longed to take them the story of Jesus. While the expedition was being conducted, the government officials, fearing a tribal war, decided that Mary would be safer in Creek Town than at Akpap. With misgivings the missionary left Okoyong for the coast town, where she spent three months with her old friends.

Her health was poor, and this, added to her concern for the bush people, detracted from the pleasure of the visit. She complained of the crowds and of "the terribly bright sky." Her Okoyong friends did not forget her; rather, they came often with gifts for their White Mother. They continued also to bring their disputes to Mary, whom they considered to be their queen, who was concerned about their temporal as well as their spiritual well-being.

Her visit was brightened by the presence at Creek Town of the Reverend W. A. Wilkie, whose father-in-law was the editor of the *Missionary Record*. Mary was delighted to fellowship with these congenial spirits, whose understanding of her work was a constant inspiration.

When the inland difficulties had been solved, Mary returned once more to Akpap's familiar duties. She had made strong friendships while on the coast, and many came to visit her as often as possible, for they had fallen under the spell of her personality. These friends sent word portraits of Mary to the homeland.

"She is usually found bareheaded and barefooted," they reported. "A twin baby is most likely in her arms and a swarm of children about her. Or she may be holding a palaver or presiding over a court session. She is always busy."

Said another, "Her power is amazing. She is really queen of the whole Okoyong district. The high commissioner and his staff leave the administration of it in her hands. She has a grip on the intricate native and political questions.

The people have a deeper reverence for her than you can imagine. When they speak of her, their tones change."

Her sacrifice for the natives was beginning to be rewarded. She had loved them through the years, prayed for them, and now they were ready to accept the Gospel she preached. "I never saw anything more beautiful," said a visitor to her hut, "than her devotion to these black children. She had a sick boy in her arms the whole time I was there. She carried him about caring for his needs, all the while directing the other work to be done."

For fifteen years she had labored alone, giving herself without reserve to God's work in Okoyong. On Saturday, August 4, 1903, the eventful fifteenth anniversary of her arrival was celebrated. Fifteen years before, on the evening of that date, Mary, weary from a day's canoe trip, soaked with rain, chilled to the bone, had landed on the Ekenge beach. Then she tramped four miles inland through the bush to find a deserted village, trudged back once more to the beach, routed the black carriers from their sleep and compelled them to carry her goods to the settlement. The following day, Sunday, Mary conducted the first Christian service at that place.

Now, fifteen years later, on that eventful Saturday evening, Mary conducted a baptismal service for seven young converts she had won by her efforts. After the baptism, the Reverend W. T. Weir, a missionary from Creek Town, assisted in organizing the first Okoyong Christian Church, into which Mary's seven converts were received as charter members. On the following Sunday morning the hall was filled to overflowing, and the missionary presented eleven children for Christian baptism, after the Lord's Supper was served for the first time to the natives and white workers who had accepted Christ as their Saviour. After the bread and wine had been served, the congregation sang Psalm 103

in their native tongue. The voices of the converted natives
joined with their black brothers in this song:

> All thine iniquities who doth
> Most graciously forgive:
> Who thy diseases all and pains
> Doth heal, and thee relieve.
>
> Who doth redeem thy life, that thou
> To death may'st not go down;
> Who thee with loving-kindness doth
> And tender mercies crown . . .

Mary was lost in revery as tears crept down her weath-
ered face and fell in great drops on the mud floor. When
the others had finished speaking, she felt she must say a
few words to her church. In a voice husky with emotion,
she charged them to build a church large enough to ac-
commodate all who would come.

"Okoyong now looks to you more than to me for proof
of the power of the Gospel," Mary said as she urged the
baptized natives to remain true to the faith which they had
received. She gave God the glory for all that had been
achieved, and recalled gratefully what He had wrought.
They had built mission houses, schools and a church. Heathen practices had been abolished. Chiefs had ceased their
fighting, and the status of women was greatly improved.

This was a wonderful day for Okoyong—a day like that
on which Mary had first arrived in the village. God had
accomplished marvels, even the impossible. The road
which the missionary had trod during that time was hard,
but it was a highway to glory. The Gospel had won its
way into the hearts of those who had been redeemed by
Jesus' death on Calvary, and Mary praised the Lord.

Her fame sounded throughout the world, but, caring
little for this recognition, she rejoiced in the God of her
salvation and determined to conquer new regions for her
Lord and King.

CHAPTER 9

TAKING CHRIST TO CANNIBAL LAND

"I feel drawn on and on by the magnetism of this land of dense darkness and mysterious, weird forests," Mary said in telling friends of her longing to open the cannibal country to the Gospel. Long she had dreamed of this, and now she was awaiting God's moment to make the venture.

The region in which she hoped to labor lay to the west of the Cross River and stretched for uncounted miles toward the Niger. Often missionaries and traders had skirted it as they traveled up the Cross River, but never had they dared to penetrate far into the forests. The Ibo tribe, numbering four million, occupied the land, but they were under the rule of the Aros clan. They lived in thirty villages near the district of Arochuku.

From here they dominated, cruelly and relentlessly, the millions who lived in the surrounding forests. The Aros were crafty and intelligent, and their strength lay in a combination of trade and religion. They traded slaves which their religion furnished, and when slaves could not be secured by trade, barter or religion, the Aros raided villages and captured the inhabitants.

In juju worship they found an almost unfailing source of slaves. The juju god was believed to live in a tree, which was considered sacred, and each village had its own god and sacred tree, over which the priests ruled. These priests became, according to tribal custom, blood brothers of the chiefs and were greatly revered.

The center of their worship was the long juju, which was about a mile from Arochuku and was reached by a winding road that penetrated a dense jungle and led at last to a gorge made silver by a stream widening into a small lake. In the center of the lake was an island on which was the long juju, represented by a shrine. Here the people came to consult the priests, and tribesmen from the surrounding villages brought their people here for worship.

As the people came to the long juju, they were seized by the priests' and chiefs' assistants. They were either sold as slaves, sacrificed in juju ceremonies or eaten by the tribesmen. Frequently entire villages came to consult the priests and were captured by the enemy. They were housed in Arochuku for a brief period and then led through the gorge, from whence they were by circuitous routes taken to slave markets or sold to slave traders. Many were eaten immediately by the cannibals.

Itu was one such market, situated on a broad beach where Enyong Creek, which drained the region occupied by the Aros, joined the Cross River. Through the forest paths the people were brought to the creek and thence to the traders' mart where they were sold. For countless years this traffic had continued, a fact apparent from the slave posts to which they were chained, the selling platforms and the huts into which the miserable victims were herded until they were sold.

Nevertheless, it was a beautiful spot, for the beach, enclosed by high bluffs, afforded a picturesque view of the rolling country which edged the jungle. The creek wound back into this land of loveliness, and heavy trees overarched the stream. Ferns, bamboos and other tropical foliage massed the banks with green. Bright birds fluttered through the jungle, and the water was covered with lilies. Boats had to push their way through the blossoms, so thick were the rose-tinted blooms.

Mary was familiar with the country, and her fame had spread to the region. Many times military expeditions had traversed the district, and she had often thought of accompanying them. She told the traders to inform the chiefs that someday she would come to their country to live. Their only answer was, "It is not safe," but Mary trusted in her Heavenly Father, and she was not afraid of the cannibals, however savage they might be and cruel the bondage of their customs. The missionary knew that as the result of a chief's death, fifty or more people had been eaten during the ceremonies, and twenty-five others, with hands tied behind their backs, had been decapitated according to burial rites, but this knowledge did not deter the missionary, for she had faced conditions only slightly less barbarous upon her arrival at Okoyong, and God had blessed her labors. She trusted Him for similar protection in this strange new land of cannibals.

She made many explorative trips up the creek to the region, and gradually acquired from officials and traders considerable information concerning the new land and its people. To the south of Enyong Creek were the Ibibios, the most degraded of the tribes, who lived in constant terror of Aros raids. Hiding deep in the forests, the people were sullen, untruthful and had a standard of life little above that of animals.

Mary considered carefully various methods of beginning her work in this new field. The missionaries of Calabar advocated that she work farther up the Cross River, where two stations had already been opened, one at Ikorofiong, above Ikunetu, the landing beach for Akpap, and the other at Unwana, still farther up the river. Mary deemed neither of these suitable as a center for operations, however, for the first was merely a trading post and the second was in a back-water district. She did not think it wise to work farther up the river where weather conditions made transportation to the coast impossible.

Ideally situated for her work was Arochuku, the chief city of the Aros and the tribes they ruled, which had the advantage of Enyong Creek and was near the Efik, Ibo and Ibibio tribes. The brave missionary determined to make her base at Itu, which was on the mouth of Enyong Creek, and later she planned to open another mission base at Arochuku and a third at Bende, a section farther inland which she desired to win.

The Calabarian missionaries again disagreed, but the decision was postponed until a permanent worker could be found for the Akpap station. Mary refused to leave these beloved people, many of whom she had won to the Saviour, until they could be properly cared for by Christian workers.

"I shall not say that I shall leave my home without a pang, but I know that I can do work which new folk cannot do, and my days of service are closing in, and I cannot build up a church in the way a minister can," she said, telling of her desire for an ordained minister to supervise the Akpap station. She had laid the foundation, on which she was convinced another could build successfully. Eminently suited to do explorative and pioneering mission work, the brave woman longed to be once more on the inland march.

Providentially, Miss Wright, of the Girls' Institute at Calabar, came to Mary's aid and asked to be sent to Akpap as an assistant, a request which was submitted to Scotland for official sanction. Meanwhile the White Queen, as the natives called her, decided to start work without an official blessing, and in January, 1903, with two boys, Esien and Effiom, and one girl, Mana, whom she had carefully trained, she loaded her canoe with supplies and set off for Itu.

Arriving there, she established temporary quarters and

left the young people to begin a school and conduct church services. Then she returned by a long and tedious route to Akpap. Here she stayed for some time. Upon her return to Itu, Mary was surprised to find how successful the venture had proved. The native workers had reached many people, young and old, at the services. On this visit Mary selected an excellent building site on the bluff above the beach.

Here, working with her own hands, Mary began to build a schoolhouse and a church. The natives assisted wholeheartedly in the labor of love. Two rooms were added to the church building as living quarters for the missionary. Once again she had planted the Christian flag in a new territory which she was to claim for the Lord Jesus Christ!

On a beautiful morning in June, 1903, after Mary had returned to Akpap, where she found that Miss Wright had received the sanction of the board, she started again for Itu, and tramped the six miles to the landing beach at Ikunetu. Here she waited to board the government launch which was to take her to Itu, but through a mistake she missed the boat and was forced to repeat the six-mile tramp through the jungle. "I am in God's hands," she said, on arriving at the mission, "and He did not mean for me to travel today. I have been kept back for some good purpose."

The following week when she again made the trip to board the launch, Colonel Montanaro, the commander of the government forces, invited her to travel under his protection, as he was enroute to Arochuku. Mary saw now why God had delayed the trip. Although she lacked necessary supplies of food and clothing, she accepted his offer to visit the center of the Aros clan that she might closely observe the juju religion.

Although as a result of a previous military expedition, the chiefs had promised to suppress the juju worship, it

continued to flourish surreptitiously. On arriving at the
town, Mary walked through the forest paths, which slaves
for centuries had trod, and came upon the scene of the long
juju, where in silence she gazed upon the human skulls,
the bones and the pots in which many bodies had been prepared for eating. She shuddered at the thought of cannibal feasts and the iniquities of savagery which abounded
here. Fervently, she asked God to grant her this region as
He had granted her Okoyong.

The people welcomed her cordially, having heard of her
fame and the work she had accomplished in the jungles.
She longed to bring the Gospel to these, Christ's "other
sheep," for whom He had shed His blood. Carefully the
brave woman studied the situation, as she prayed that the
homeland church would permit her to win this territory for
Christ. Finally, after promising to come again and open a
school, she returned to Akpap, where she soon received
word from the authorities that it would be impossible at
the time to open work at Arochuku.

Although this news burdened Mary's heart, it did not deter her, for she trusted in Christ who was able to "do ex-
ceeding abundantly" above all she was able to ask or think.
She had asked the Heavenly Father to give her a mission
station where His Gospel might be preached to the Aros,
and she was confident that He would grant her request. She
set out for Arochuku with some of her boys, now old enough
to assist with schoolwork and church services, and upon her
arrival at Amasu, a small settlement nearer the creek than
Arochuku, she opened a school. It was soon filled with boys
and girls, "thirsty for book and the loving God."

When Mary prepared to return to the Akpap station,
after having left workers to care for the school and conduct the work, the tribesmen crowded around her and

pleaded, "Come again soon, White Ma. If you do not care for us, who will care for us?"

As the canoe skimmed gently down the stream, Mary praised God for permitting her to open this new field to the Gospel. Suddenly a canoe appeared. In it was a native. "I have been waiting for you. My master at Akani Obio sent me to waylay you and bring you to his house," he said as he handed her a letter.

Astonished, the missionary read the message and ordered her canoe to follow his. They soon entered a beautiful tributary creek, which brought them to a popular trading post. Here Mary was greeted by a handsome young man, who, with his well-dressed and dignified black wife, led the missionary to a European-type house, which was attractively furnished. Amazed, the White Ma listened to his pathetic story.

He was Onoyom Iya Nya, the president of the native court and the chief of the district. He told Mary that as a boy he had heard the Gospel story from a missionary whom he had served as a guide. He was severely punished for this by his tribe, and consequently grew up as a heathen and participated in the Arochuku cannibal feasts. But he never forgot what the missionary had told him about Christ. Disturbed, he had sought to find by witchcraft the person who had placed the misfortune upon him, but he met, instead, a missionary who was not faithful to his calling.

"How do you know it is not the God of the white man who is angry with you? He is all-powerful," said the man, and Onoyom had asked eagerly, "How can I find this God?"

"I am not worthy to say. But find the White Ma who goes to Itu and she will tell you."

Accordingly, he had sent his servants at various times to search for Mary as she went up and down Enyong Creek, but he had not found her until this day. Mary listened to his story as tears of joy rolled down her cheeks. Other members of the household came to see her and she told them of Jesus and His power to save them. She read from the Bible, prayed with the people, and promised to repeat the visit.

Mary's soul was stirred as she pondered the new work. She was grateful for the opening at Itu and Amasu, which lay but a short distance from Arochuku, where she hoped to conquer the cannibals for Christ. She desired to yield her Akpap station to an ordained minister and take Miss Wright to Itu with her, for she realized that the Enyong Creek region would provide ample work for the laborers.

Mary made trips from Akpap to Itu and Amasu, and stopped along the creek to bring the message of salvation at isolated huts and small settlements. Often she slept on mud floors and ate yams and native fruits that she might tell the benighted cannibals of Christ's redeeming love. At both Itu and Amasu the work progressed rapidly under the Father's blessings. More than three hundred intelligent, neatly-dressed natives attended the Itu services in a church they had built.

At Amasu, on a wet August day, Mary had the joy of seeing sixty-eight attend the school, and many of them were already able to read.

As she watched the natives build her six-room house at Itu, she said, "I am afraid it is too much work for you. It is too big." It was to be one of the finest homes the missionary had occupied, but the natives declared, when she suggested that the task was too large, "No, it is not too much. Nothing is too much to do for you. We shall do it."

On another occasion a native woman knelt at her feet and insisted on washing them in hot water. Touched by this act of devotion, Mary thanked her for the deed, and the woman replied, "I have been so afraid, Ma, that you

would think us unworthy of a teacher and take her away.
I could not live again in darkness. I pray all the time. I
lay my basket down and pray on the road."

Mary also found strength and comfort in prayer, and she
often wrote to her friends, "Prayer can do anything." She
had tested the power of Christ and found it sufficient for
any difficulty.

One day Mary conceived a daring plan, and considered
the possibility of freeing herself entirely from the mission
board and testing God's promises.

"I think it an open secret that for many years the workers
have felt that our methods and modes were very far from
adequate to undertake the needs of our immense field," she
wrote to the Calabar missionaries. "The scattered broken
units into which our African populations are divided, their
various jujus and superstitions, which segregate even houses
of any common village, make it necessary for us to do
more than merely pay an occasional visit, even if that results in the building of a school or a church. For the last
decade, the nearer reaches of the river have occupied a
great deal of my thought, but from various causes no sort
of supervision at all adequate has suggested itself."

Mary was preparing a proposal which, instead of cul-
minating in a furlough, due on January 2, 1904, after five
years in the jungle, resulted in a six-month leave.

"I propose to ask leave from the station for six months,
during which time I should in a very easy way try to
keep up an informal system of itinerating between Okoyong and Amasu. Already I have seen a church and a
dwelling house built at Itu, and a school and a couple of
rooms at Amasu. I have visited several towns of Enyong
and have found good enough accommodations.

"I shall find my own canoe and crew, and shall stay at
any given place any length of time the circumstances sug-

gest . . . and members of my family shall help in the elementary teaching in the schools."

The missionary proposed thus to superintend the various smaller schools she had established at Idot and Eki, but planned to "reside at Itu as the base, working the Creek and Enyong towns on the way to the farthest base at Amasu, reside there, or itinerate from there among the Aros in an easy way, and back again by Creek and Itu home."

She asked that an assistant be sent to aid Miss Wright at Akpap, so that Mary would be free to conduct the new work in the jungle. She also sought Miss Wright's assistance in the labors among the cannibals so that she herself might have more time for pioneer work in the outlying districts.

Mary desired that the project at Itu be conducted as a "European station," so that the various tribes could be reached from this base of operations. "As a natural and strategic point in the business conduct of our mission, Itu is incomparable," she wrote. "It was not without reason that it became the slave mart . . . the gateway to the Aros and the Ibibios, holding Enyong, and being just a day's journey from what must ever be our base, namely, the seaport of the ocean steamers, having waterway all the year around and a good beach front, it is the natural point at which our up- and down-river work should converge."

The White Queen of Okoyong outlined a complex plan of activities, although she was in her fifty-sixth year and had endured extreme suffering and privations. Now she was planning a task which would challenge even a younger and stronger worker. She did not draw back nor flinch. The word "doubt" was not in her vocabulary. With Livingstone she declared, "Anywhere—provided it be forward," and added ". . . among the cannibals."

God had given her an opportunity to reach the fierce cannibals, and she was willing to die in the attempt to bring the Gospel to them. Faith and prayer had always sustained her. With these two allies she could not fail.

Chapter 10

GYPSYING WITH THE GOSPEL

Mary's desire to go on a "gypsying tour of the jungle," as she spoke of it, was destined to bring memorable results for God's kingdom. The White Queen was aware of the dangers she faced, but was willing to undertake the journey that other tribes and peoples might hear the Gospel. When the request went forward to the board, the answer was delayed, but the missionary was accustomed to such periods of waiting.

Mary longed intensely to enter new regions and she decided to invite the Wilkies and Miss Wright to accompany her on a trip through her territory that they might see what God had wrought among the cannibals. The Calabar workers were more than willing to be her guests in cannibal land and Mary included in the party several of her black children.

The travelers first visited Itu, where they met Colonel Montanaro. Their next stop was at Akani Obio, where Chief Onoyom entertained them in sumptuous jungle style. He was eager to have Mary visit his section with the Gospel. The party next went to Amasu, and finally reached other villages in and around Arochuku and the scene of the long juju. On the return trip they stopped at many smaller settlements where the people were eager to learn "book."

Arriving at Akpap, Mary found that the board had given its long-awaited sanction to the jungle trip, but she would have to pay her own expenses during this time. "I have no object on earth," she said, "but to get my food and raiment, which are of the plainest, and to bring up my bairns." When traveling time arrived she was thrilled at the prospect of going where Christian workers' feet had never trod.

"It seems strange to be starting with a family on a gypsy life in a canoe, but God will take care of us. Whether I shall find His place for me up-river or whether I shall come back to my own people again, I do not know. He knows, and that is enough."

Preparation for the trip demanded a journey to Duke Town, where Mary relinquished her legal duties and purchased supplies. Here she met the Reverend J. K. MacGregor, principal of the Hope Waddell Institute, which she had helped to establish. MacGregor pictures Mary as a "slim figure of middle height, with fine eyes full of power. It is wonderful to sit and listen to her talking, for she is most fascinating, and besides being a humorist, is a fine source of information on mission history and Efik customs."

On a July morning the little party set out for the Akpap landing, whence they would venture into the savage wilderness. In the entire history of Christian exploration there had never been a stranger expedition: a frail, elderly woman, black crewmen and a group of dusky children, whose purpose was to spread life-changing news. Eventually the party landed at Itu. A government official says concerning Mary:

"What a picture she presented! Here was a native hut with a few of the barest necessities of furniture. She was sitting on a chair, rocking a tiny baby, while five others, wrapped in bits of brown paper and newspapers, were quietly sleeping in other parts of the room. How she managed to look after all these children and to do the colossal work she did passes my comprehension."

God had caused her work to prosper. The Itu congregation, deep in cannibal land, consisted of three hundred people, and many others requested help. From Ibibio, southward, the natives sent messages to Mary requesting a teacher. A chief sent this urgent message: "It is **not** book I want. _I want God!_"

Chief Onoyom of Akani Obio was unrelenting in his pleas. "We have three in hand for a teacher. Some of the boys have already finished the books Mr. Wilkie gave us. We can do no more until you send us help." Fifteen young men from Okoyong declared that the missionaries at Akpap had left them and there was no one to take their place. "We have no Ma now," they reported sadly.

Mary spent the night in prayer, calling upon the Almighty to supply the workers. "Oh, Britain, surfeited with privilege, tired of Sabbath and church, would that you could send over to us what you are throwing away!" she said. Mary prayed at night and worked tirelessly during the day. She found that the house at Itu was unfinished, and with her own hands she mixed the cement for the floors while Janie, whom she now called Jean, did the whitewashing. When asked how she learned to make cement, Mary replied:

"I just stir it like porridge, then turn it out, smooth it with a stick, and all the time keep praying, 'Lord, here's the cement. If it be to Thy glory, set it,' and it has never once gone wrong."

Nor did she neglect to make daily visits and solve the problems which arose among Itu's cannibals. Said a visitor who came to see Mary, "We visited women in their homes . . . had evening prayers in such yards as the owners were willing . . . One person brought a story of an unjust divorce, another was sick, and one came with a primer for a reading lesson. Another was accused of debt and wanted Ma to vouch for his innocence. Another had been cheated in a land case. All found a ready listener . . . and none went away without hearing of the salvation God had prepared for them."

Progress in God's work was steady. Chief Onoyom remained steadfast in his faith and built a church. He horrified the people by cutting down the juju tree for use in the building. "The juju will not permit it!" they cried, but the chief declared, "God is stronger than juju." A reverent, well-dressed group attended the dedicatory services. One found it difficult to believe that only two years earlier the town was known only to traders and the people indulged in heathen practices.

At Arochuku a school was being built, and despite her years, Mary helped to construct the mud walls. A church building was also erected, and the missionary was no longer forced to conduct outdoor services.

At other settlements along Enyong Creek, schoolhouses and churches were built and congregations organized. At the Mission Council meeting held at Calabar in 1905, the brave missionary told of the work accomplished. At Itu a church and schoolhouse had been built; services were held and a dayschool conducted. At Arochuku, a schoolhouse had been erected, and at Oko, Akani Obio, Odot and Asang, buildings were already completed and congregations gathered in them regularly. The Council, thrilled by the glowing report of salvation among the cannibals, voted that Mary's "gypsying furlough" be extended six months, but again they stipulated that she must bear the financial burden unassisted.

A question troubled Mary. Should she continue the work up Enyong Creek, or turn her attention southward to the Ibibios, the most degraded people in the region? "The lower in the scale of humanity, the more they need help," was the argument which resulted in her decision to work among the Ibibios.

Meanwhile the Mission Committee in Scotland established a medical base at Itu, with a Cape Town physician, Dr.

Robertson, as its head. Plans were made for a new mission house, a hospital and even a motor launch. The dispensary and the hospital were to be named in the missionary's honor, "The Mary Slessor Mission Hospital."

"It seems like a fairy tale," she said when informed that money had been provided for the venture, "and I don't know just what to say. I can just look up into the blue sky and say, 'Even so, Father; in good and ill, let me live and be worthy of it all.' It is a grand gift and I am so glad for my people."

Now that the problem of Itu had been miraculously solved, she turned her attention to Ibibio, where the government was opening roads and establishing courts. Officials and traders were constant visitors at her Itu home, and earnestly sought her advice regarding people and customs in this cannibal region. Chiefs also asked her if the white man's invasion of their land was detrimental.

"Get a bicycle, Ma," said an official. "Here is the road. Come as far as you can. And we'll soon have a motorcar for you."

She made her decision in 1905, and took her twelve-year-old boy, Etim, along, for he could read and she needed his aid. Traveling inland five miles to Ikotobong, she started a school and organized a small congregation.

"It is my hope that it will be the first of a chain of stations stretching across the country. The old chief is pleased. He told me that the future, the mystery of things, was too much for him and that he would welcome the light. The people are to give Etim food and I will pay him five shillings a month for his mother . . ."

The boy proved to be an excellent teacher, and soon had organized a class consisting of fifty children. Mary and the natives began a building program, but the missionary longed to enter a new section with the old, old story of

redemption. When the district commissioner of Ikot Expene, an inland government center, gave her a bicycle,
she decided that it was God's will that she learn to ride it.

"Fancy an old woman like me on a cycle! The new road
makes it easy to ride and I'm running up and down and
taking a new work in a village two miles off. It has done
me all the good in the world and I will soon be able to
undertake more work."

The plight of the native women in Ibibio was appalling.
They were chattel, degraded, pawns of the harem master,
and if unmarried, they could legally be raped, tortured,
assaulted or injured. They had become merchandise of
barter, and Mary's loving heart was burdened with the desire to help them.

Accordingly, she planned to build a home for girls, waifs,
orphans, twins and their mothers and refugees from harems.
She also desired to organize a school where various trades
and skills could be taught. All the women had a knowledge
of farming, and many knew how to weave baskets and
make simple footwear.

As the missionary traveled about, she looked for a suitable place, where there was fertile land and pure water, to
grow the products which would provide a large part of
their income. She also sought a location near markets or
roads that led to them. Awaiting God's time, she spoke
to friends about the project and wrote to the missionary
board regarding her plans.

In April, 1906, her extended gypsy furlough was to end
and she must return to Akpap, for the Mission Council expected her to work at a specified station. She rebelled at
the thought of settling in one place and said, "There is an
impelling power behind me and I dare not look backward.
Even if it costs my connection with the church of my
heart's love, I feel I must go forward." Studying the situa-

tion, she later remarked, "I am not enthusiastic over church methods. I would not mind cutting the rope and going adrift with my bairns, and I can earn our bite and something more."

This led Ma Slessor to consider taking a government position or opening a store. Finally she presented a summary of the matter to the mission board. Recounting God's blessings at Itu and the surrounding country, she said:

"In all this how plainly God has been leading me. I had not a thought of such things in my lifetime . . . and yet my steps have been led, apart from any plan of mine, right to the line of God's planning for the country. First Itu, and then Creek, then back from Aro, where I had set my heart, to a solitary wilderness of the most forbidding description, where the silence of the bush had never been broken, and here before three months are past there are miles of road . . . being worked on . . . as even a novelist could imagine.

"And the Minutes say I am to return to Akpap in April. No place on earth is so dear to my heart, but to leave these hordes of untamed, unwashed, unlovely savages and withdraw the little sunlight that has begun to flicker out over its darkness—I dare not think of it!"

The board had made this decision, but Mary could not feel, even after much prayer, that the plan was God's will. The missionary knew that her age did not favor this "gypsy" life, and that walking would be difficult, but she trusted that God would solve the problem.

"Whether the church permits or not, I feel I must stay here and even go farther on as the roads are made. I cannot walk now, nor dare I do anything trifling with my health . . . but if the roads are all the easy gradients of those already made, I can get four wheels made and set a box on them, and the children can draw me . . .

"I dare not go back. I shall rather take the risk of finding my own fare."

The church eventually consented, and Mary offered to build, at her expense, a station among the Ibibios, if there was no money in the homeland treasury. John Rankin had been sent to analyze the situation and reported that "close to Arochuku within a circle the diameter of which is less than three miles, there are nineteen large towns. I visited sixteen of these, each of which is larger than Creek Town . . . The majority are anxious for help . . . already many have begun to try to live in God's fashion!"

Even the head chief of all Aros, formerly in control of the long juju, was eager that mission work be conducted in the region, and had announced to the other chiefs his intention to rule according to God's ways. He eagerly requested that the missionaries come to his people.

Rankin's report so aroused the board's enthusiasm that they offered to finance the work Mary had planned and even appointed Rankin to superintend the stations, both at Itu and Arochuku, "where the chief offers to build a house for any missionary who will come."

This freed Mary and made it possible for her to follow the gleam which was luring her into new regions. In May of that year, God provided miraculously for her support. She was appointed by the government to take charge of court affairs in the Ibibio district as she had done formerly at Okoyong. Court was held at Ikotobong, where clerical work and the hearing of cases increased the frail missionary's duties. This work permitted her to witness the lowest moral conditions she had yet encountered.

"God help those poor helpless women," she wrote to a friend. "What a crowd of people I have had today and how debased . . . like brutes in regard to women. I have had a murder, an essere (poison bean) case, a suicide, a

man branding his slave wife all over face and body, a
man with a gun who had shot four persons—it is all horrible."

Three local chiefs and a jury assisted Mary in trying
the cases, but her verdict was supreme. By her just de-
crees, motivated by Christian love, she did much here also
to prevent twin murders. Gospel influence was at work,
and an official reported, "The result is a sign of the civil-
izing influence working through the court by that admirable
lady, Miss Slessor."

Said the natives, "Her Master was beside her, and His
Spirit guarded her." An official added, "She combines most
happily kindliness and severity, and I cannot imagine any
native trying to take advantage of her kindness and her
great-hearted love for the people." Visitors, expecting to
find a mannish woman because of her many courageous
deeds, were surprised to see that she was truly feminine,
"a true woman with a heart full of motherly affection."

Mary greeted mail eagerly, for she was always interested
in the homeland. Papers from Scotland were welcome, for
they brought news of the outside world. She refused to
reduce her work to routine. One hour she was discussing
a political situation with a visiting district commissioner;
the next she was supervising the construction of a house.

"Late one evening," reported a visitor at her station, "I
heard a great deal of talking and commotion. I went to
see what was going on and there was Ma making cement
and the bairns spreading it on the floor with their hands
in the candlelight."

While walking one Sunday, she came to a government
road camp where the natives were gathered around their
huts. She began to chat with them, and told them the
story of the lost sheep. Her language, now as always, was
so graphic and so close to the vernacular that the natives

listened intently. Most of them had never heard of a God of love.

In this manner Mary conducted her mission work among the cannibals. She approached them as equals, told them of Jesus' death for them, and later, when the blessed seed bore fruit, she opened schools and churches for the natives. Mary Slessor, the White Ma, the White Queen of the Okoyong tribes, had a vision of the Gospel's transforming power even among the most degraded.

Although she was constantly occupied with routine duties, she did not forget her dreams. She envisioned a rest home for missionaries, a place where they could spend week-ends or convalesce. One day Mary received a hundred-dollar check from a friend, and used this as the nest egg for the home. She selected a site midway between Itu and Ikotobong on Enyong Creek, high above the lowlands which extended on one side toward Arochuku and on the other far into Ibibio and its plains. Ground was soon cleared and a small semi-European house begun.

During most of 1906 the missionary's health was in a precarious state, and the government doctor warned that if she was to continue her work she must recuperate in Scotland. Dreading to leave her beloved work, she rallied briefly and said to the physician, "It looks as if God has forbidden my going. Does this appear as if He could do without me? Oh, dear me, poor old lady, how little you can do! But I can at least keep a door open."

By 1907, unable to walk more than a few steps, she was carried from place to place. Her brave spirit yielded and she decided to return to the homeland.

"Oh, the dear homeland!" she exclaimed, her eyes filled with tears. "Shall I really be there and worship in the churches again? How I long for a look at a winter landscape, to feel the cold wind, and the frost in the cart ruts

. . . to take a back seat in a church and hear without a care of my own the congregation singing, and hear how they preach and pray and rest their souls in the hush and solemnity."

These wishes were to be fulfilled, except her desire "to feel the cold wind," for she left in May, taking with her six-year-old Dan, one of her boys. The government officials' kindness in preparing for her leave caused Mary to say, "God must repay these men, for I cannot. He will not forget they did it to a child of His, unworthy though she be."

CHAPTER 11

SPENDING HERSELF FOR THE GOSPEL

Mary Slessor cared little for self; the Gospel was her primary interest. When she arrived in Scotland, she was a wrinkled, shining-eyed old lady, who had given herself without stint and reserve for Christ's kingdom. His cause was her joy. Her Saviour had died for her salvation, and she had been willing to die that Africa might have the light. With little Dan by her side to remind her of the natives whom she had left behind, she soon regained her health sufficiently to undertake a speaking deputation among the churches.

The earnest missionary had inspired people to contribute to her work. Her constant plea was, "Send us workers for dark Africa." She promised, "If I can get the board to send one or more workers, I shall give half of my salary to add to theirs and will give the house and find the servants."

She visited familiar scenes of her childhood at Dundee, where celestial light first shone into her girlhood heart. She also met various officials of the Mission Board and attended conferences. Her personal message aroused the people's faith and love to such an extent that they gladly contributed to the causes she represented.

Her major aim was to finance the industrial home for women which she had planned. From May until October she challenged the home church with the call of Christ's "other African sheep, not of this fold." Sad rumors had come to her that Janie, or Jean, as she called her, was failing in her Christian example, and Mary decided that she must know the facts regarding her first bairn, the little twin whom she had long ago rescued from death.

"I am foolish, I know," Mary said when she asked to be returned to the field in October, 1907, "but I just feel homeless without kith or kin, a poor solitary with only memories."

She realized that if Janie had failed, all her hopes would be ruined, so, with a hurried farewell, she sailed once more for Calabar and the redeemed cannibals she had won for her Master. When she reached her inland post, she again resumed the usual routine of duties, presided at court, often eight hours a day, and supervised her home. On Sundays she conducted a half-dozen or a dozen services in the surrounding villages, in which the people lived with whom she worked during the week. On some of these trips she brought back children to join her already "overstuffed" household. Energetically she plastered, painted, whitewashed and subdued the ever-encroaching jungle.

Her health, temporarily improved by her Scotland furlough, soon failed and her strength waned. Nevertheless she could write, "Still, the bursts of glory that come between the clouds are a rich provision for our frail and sensitive lives."

The long hours of unremitting, exhaustive toil, the primitive living quarters, the lack of nourishing food—these caused her letters to include such notes as these: "I am tired, tired . . . My mother went home eighteen years ago on the passage of the Old Year, so it is rather lonely tonight with so many memories. But He has never failed, and He is all-sufficient."

Her eyes were growing dim, but spiritually she could see clearly that the Lord was blessing her work. Stations along Enyong Creek prospered, and where four years before there had been no Christians and no missionary activity, now there were two hundred faithful converted blacks who contributed more than a thousand dollars to God's work.

Two problems troubled Mary. The first was the demand for a decision concerning the home for women and girls which would enable them to be self-supporting. Friends contributed money liberally and officials promised to purchase all the products she could produce. Finally she selected a site near by. Enthusiastically she planted fruit trees—guavas, pawpaws, mangoes, avocadoes, bananas, pineapples and other fruits. She planned also to produce rubber and cocoa, and later she raised cattle to make the venture more certain of success.

She was also considering a second project: she desired to move some distance up the Enyong, to the west of Arochuku and north of Ibibio, where she was now laboring. She had selected one of Nigeria's most degraded sections—far more degraded than Ibibio when she first settled there. Before her furlough, a group of natives from this section begged her to bring the Gospel to them. "We have heard of the Great White Mother and want to become God-men," they declared earnestly.

They had come from an important slave center called Ikpe. After the furlough they repeated their request, and Mary could not refuse to grant it. Accordingly, she decided to make the two-day canoe trip to their settlement. She found Ikpe to be a large and prosperous town, where many types of people mingled. Morally they were degraded. After studying the settlement, she decided that it was a strategic center for Christian work, for it provided her access to several tribes and opened an inland contact with Arochuku.

Already those who wanted to become Christians had begun to build a small church building, to which they added two rooms for the missionary's convenience. Here Mary held services while a reverent audience listened for the first time to the message of salvation. Immediately after the service she decided that it was God's will for her to move to this new locality.

Upon her return home she experienced, as she expressed it, her "ups and downs of sickness." She spent much of her time supervising the women's home. Finally another deputation arrived from Ikpe, and Mary made additional trips to the village, accompanied by other missionaries. Meanwhile she was trying to free herself from several burdens, among which was her court work, which she discontinued in November, 1909, having sent her resignation to the government.

When it looked as if she would be free to undertake the new inland venture, she became severely ill in 1910, and the government sent its official automobile to take her to the Mary Slessor Hospital at Itu, where she was nursed back to health. Then followed a period of convalescence at Duke Town, and the government sent its launch, the *Maple Leaf,* for the down-river journey.

"I am doing nothing but eating," she wrote to friends, "and shedding my buttons all over the place. I am being spoiled in a new atmosphere, not of tender love, but of literacy and cultured Christian grace and winsomeness, and it has been as perfect a fortnight as I ever spent."

Having regained her health, Mary returned by government boat, to her inland post, where she at once took up the task of spreading the Gospel. Before leaving for Ikpe, she could not be content without establishing a station at Ikot Expene, farther inland from Ikotobong, where she was located. When her strength permitted, she bicycled into the bush toward the place, selecting possible locations for schools and churches along the way, talking to chiefs, and laying the foundation for future outstations.

Nor had she forgotten Ikpe on the upper reaches of Enyong Creek where natives were hungering for the Gospel. They were holding services themselves, even though they knew only the rudimentary truths of Christianity. Their desire was their strength, and God blessed the light they had received. They believed firmly that when the White Ma returned she would tell them more fully about Him. A native teacher from another station, who had received a little training, taught the people what he knew concerning the Gospel.

"Oh, why cannot the church send two workers there? Why don't they use the money on hand for the purpose? If the wherewithal should fail at the end of two years, let them take my salary. I shall only be too glad to live on native food with my bairns." Thus spoke Mary.

At once she began to collect the necessary building materials and other essentials. To friends she said, "I am entering in the dark. As to how and where and when I am to manage, I do not know, but my mind is at perfect peace about it, and I am not afraid to go. God will carry it through. The pillar of fire leads." She was sustained by faith in God and a sense of the Divine Presence in the venture.

Finally God's moment came, and Mary set out for Ikpe only to find that her house was too near the mosquito-laden creek. Gladly she accepted the place, however, and began the task of clearing it. On three sides were stately palms, which added to the beauty of the location.

"These palms are my first joy in the morning when the dawn comes up, pearly gray in the mist and fine rain, fresh and cool and beautiful," she said.

The missionary resumed the strength-sapping routine she had known among the Ibibios and formerly at Okoyong. She silenced mobs, calmed bickering chiefs, held palaver with the crowds and on Sundays conducted services. When a smallpox epidemic broke out, the natives were afraid of the "white man's juju," as they called the vaccination, and excitement prevailed. Guns and swords appeared and only through the White Ma's diplomacy and prayer was the riot subdued.

"It is a real life I am living now," she wrote, "not all preaching and holding meetings, but rather a life and an atmosphere which the people can touch and live in and be made willing to believe in when the higher truths are brought before them ... The excitement and surprises and novel situations would not, however, need to be continuous, as they wear and fray the body, fret the spirit and rob one of sleep and restfulness of soul."

She spoke of herself as "the broken reed upon which they lean."

Mary desired to retain contact with her former Ikotobong headquarters, and made frequent canoe trips which exhausted her frail body. One of these journeys required thirteen hours in the rude native canoe. When she arrived at the landing beach late in the evening, accompanied by a native girl and an infant, Mary set out for her home carrying a heavy box of chickens, while the girl transported the baby. When they reached their destination the missionary was too exhausted even to remove her clothes; throwing herself wearily on the bed, she sank into a fitful sleep.

Despite ill health and constant attacks of fever, Mary could write, "My heart is singing all the time to Him whose love and tender mercy crown all the days." During 1911 a tornado struck her house at Use, one of the outstation abodes. She repaired the damage with her own hands, thereby straining herself. This exertion resulted in a heart ailment, followed by raging fever and delirium. The missionary, however, refused to abandon the work and she continued to teach school and conduct divine worship on Sundays. After a busy and trying Sunday she said to friends, "I had a grand day notwithstanding intense weakness."

A new physician, Dr. Hitchcock, took Dr. Robertson's place at the Slessor Hospital, and, concerned about Mary's health, he sent messengers to her when she stayed in a distant town. Once or more weekly he made the trip to Use that he might personally observe the state of her health.

One day Dr. Hitchcock discovered this entry in her diary: "Market Morning—have only 3d in cash . . . sent it with 2 Ikpats [the first Efik schoolbook] and New Testament to buy food, and sold all three books for 6d. Got five small yams, oil and shrimps, with pepper and a few small fresh fish."

When the doctor discovered the entry, he at once forbade her to go again to Ikpe or bicycle anywhere. He insisted, furthermore, that she spend much time resting. The following Sunday, however, she disregarded his orders and conducted services, after which she found herself near collapse.

Upon his return the doctor ordered her to bed "until I think you are well enough to get up." Mary agreed meekly and said of him, "He is very strict. But he is a dear man. Thank God for him." When orders came for her to eat meat twice a day, she replied, "I'm not a meat-eater," but the doctor threatened her with an enforced rest at Duke Town if she did not obey.

Mary merely laughed and declared, "I've all my plans made and I must not draw a salary and not do something for it."

Eventually the doctor ordered her to the Slessor Hospital for a rest, as she insisted upon supervising household affairs at the station. She suffered raging fevers as a result of her tireless labors. Mary relented, saying, "Life is hardly worth living, but I'm doing what I can to help him to help me, so that I can be fit again for another spell of work."

The Christian Ikpe natives sent a delegation asking when she would be back. The doctor replied, "Seven weeks," but Mary countered, "I may run up sooner than that. I'm quite well if he would only believe it." Near the end of 1911 she was able to leave the hospital, and escaped, as she wrote, "out of the clutches of the dearest and cleverest and most autocratic mission doctor that ever lived."

Released from the hospital, which to her had been a prison, Mary hastened to her friends at Ikpe. The Calabar Council had promised that two helpers would be given to her, but the group thought it wise before sending them to secure a medical report on living conditions and the location of the missionaries. The report was unfavorable; consequently the workers were denied and Mary was forced to carry the burden alone. Her health was so precarious that she referred to herself as a "sputtering candle," which caused Calabarian and Scottish friends to urge her to take a long-earned furlough.

While considering the possibility of a furlough, Mary decided to have a "box on wheels" constructed, as she could no longer make bicycle trips into the bush. However, friends in Scotland, hearing of the idea, promptly sent her a cart which could be wheeled by two boys or girls. This caused Mary to dismiss the thought of a furlough in Scotland.

"Instead of going home as I had planned, in order to get strength and a wider range of work, I shall stay on and enjoy the privilege of going over ground impossible for my poor limbs."

Immediately Mary began to execute the plans she had made before leaving Ibibio for outstations to be established between her various headquarters. A government road was being opened between Ikpe and Ikot Expene, and Mary intended to construct along it a network of schools and churches which would extend throughout the Ibibio territory.

Her strength did not keep pace with her vision, for the recurrence of her heart ailment made it necessary for her to rest. Had there been anyone to relieve her, she would have taken an immediate furlough in the homeland.

"We were never so shorthanded," she wrote, "and I can do what others cannot, what, indeed, medical opinion would not allow them to try. No one meddles with me and I slip along and do my work with less expenditure of strength than many."

Mary knew that if she took a furlough at that time her work would virtually cease, for there was no one to manage the outstations nor occupy her headquarters. Her heart was in Africa, and she longed to spend her remaining days in this land. However, the thought of seeing her Scottish friends again awakened fond memories.

"These little glimpses, like pictures, of home and the old country, of family ties and love, make me long for just one long summer day in the midst, if only as an onlooker, and for the touch of loving hands and a bit of family worship in our tongue, and maybe a Sabbath service thrown in with a psalm and an old-fashioned tune, and then I should feel ready for a long spell of work.

"But I should fret if it should take me away from this . . . my real life. This life is full . . . and is a precious possession . . . I should choose this life if I had to begin again; only, I should try to live it to better purpose."

Mary could never get Africa out of her heart. It was here she had first landed almost thirty-six years earlier, a young woman, full of strength and inspired by a heavenly vision.

As no help came, she worked until the summer of 1912, and the opportunity for a furlough passed. In September she completed thirty-six years on the field and said whimsically, "I'm lame and feeble and foolish. The wrinkles are wonderful—no concertina is so wonderfully folded and convoluted. I'm a wifie, vera little buikit, but I grip on well, nonetheless." An old doctor friend said to her, "Aye, you are a strong woman. You ought to have been dead by ordinary rule long ago. Anyone else would."

Mary's friends feared for her health, and since she could not make the trip to Scotland in the winter, the mission board received the suggestion that she be sent on an expense-paid trip to the Canary Islands for recuperation. Miss Cook, a board member, said to Mary, "I believe in taking care of the Lord's servant. I am afraid you do not fully realize how valuable you are to all of us, the church at home and the church in Nigeria."

This filled Mary's eyes with tears, but she saw into eternity. *Perhaps it is a duty to take care of my health in the interests of the church,* she thought. This caused her to leave her Ikpe work and go to Duke Town, where she could consult her old friend and senior medical officer, Dr. Adams, who advised her to take the trip to the Canary Islands.

"Others need the holiday more than I," she said when the doctor and her friends urged her to go. "It is extravagance." It might be a good investment which will enable me to do more work for Christ's kingdom—this thought culminated in her decision to visit the islands. She had given God her best for thirty-six years, and unceasingly she had spent her life in His service. Now she asked Him to touch her frail body that she might be enabled to give her beloved natives in Nigeria a few more years of Christian service.

CHAPTER 12

EXCHANGING CALABAR'S CROSS FOR
HEAVEN'S CROWN

The vacation in the Canary Islands proved a blessing. Mary regained her strength and recovered remarkably. In this beautiful land she was not wearied by conferences, committee meetings and court cases. She reveled in the beauty of flowers and sky and sea.

"In the silence and beauty and peace," she said to a friend, "I commune with God. He is so near and so dear. Oh, if I can only get another day in which to work! I hope it will be more full of earnestness and blessing than the past . . . All are kind—the manager's family, the doctor. It is simply wonderful. I can't say anything else."

Meanwhile, she was influencing other guests at the hotel, one of whom wrote, "She made many friends . . . The entire negation of self which she evinced is remarkable . . . A lady was heard to say, 'Well, after talking to Miss Slessor, I am converted to foreign missions.' "

Blessed with health, she returned to Duke Town where a medical examination revealed that she was as sound as an elephant's ivory tusk. Said the doctor, "You are good for many years, if you will only take care." This need for precaution irked the missionary. Never in her life had she been content to "twiddle her thumbs," and now that she was back on African soil, her alert mind teemed with plans. She must work for the Master.

On this return journey to cannibal land, Mary's faith was stronger and more dominant than ever. She realized as never before that she must labor in the Master's strength. In the battle she was to wage, prayer was to be her unfailing weapon.

"My life is one long, daily, hourly record of answered prayer," she wrote a Scottish friend. "For physical health, for mental overstrain, for guidance given marvelously, for enmity to the Gospel subdued, for food provided at the exact hour needed, for everything that goes to make up life and my poor service.

"I can testify with a full and often wonder-stricken awe that I . . . know God answers prayer. I have proved during the long decades alone, as far as man's help is concerned, that God answers prayer . . . It is the very atmosphere in which I live and breathe and have my being, and it makes life grand and free and a million times worth living. I can give no other testimony. I am sitting alone here on a log among a company of natives. My children are a testimony that God answers prayer. Natives are crowding on the bush road to attend palavers and I am at perfect peace, far from my own countrymen and conditions because I know God answers prayer. Food is scarce just now. We live from hand to mouth. We have not more than will be our breakfast today, but I know we shall be fed, for God answers prayer."

For the next two years she divided her attention between Use and Ikpe, where labors engulfed her. Occasionally she used a canoe for journeys, and at other times the government launch was available, but more often she was pushed about in the two-wheeled cart by her native children. At Ikpe, where the work was still in the pioneering stage, she was forced to do much of the building herself. She supervised the making of cement, whitewashed the walls of the house and yet she did every task in a spirit of gratitude and praise to her Heavenly Father.

The labor was intense, for she continued to battle heathenism, cannibalism in the juju worship and fought constantly to abolish the custom of murdering twins. This tired her, and she tried so desperately to maintain an emotional balance that even her homeland letters were neglected.

"I counted today eight hundred women and girls running to get to the best places at the fishing grounds after the men left. And this is but a fraction of the vast number of women here. But what can I do with supervision of school, church, dispensary and household? I cannot do this work properly. And the infant churches need so much to be instructed.

"The adults are illiterate and the young need systematic teaching of the Bible. They are an emotional people and are fain to keep to speaking and singing and long prayers, and the sterner, practical side of Christianity is set aside. They are children in everything that matters, and when we have led them to Christ, we are apt to forget how much more they need in order to make a strong, upright, ethical character on which to build a nation."

It was now eight years since the missionary had left Akpap and the beloved people of Okoyong. A new church was being completed in her former location, and the resident missionaries, the Misses Ames and Ramsay, invited Mary to attend the dedicatory and opening services. The desire to see familiar faces—faces she had loved through the years—resulted in her decision to accept the invitation, and, as usual, she took the children with her.

It was a glorious July day in 1913 when Mary arrived for the event. From far and near the people thronged to see their Mother. The place was as busy as a market. There was much talk and excitement. The children whom Mary brought with her aroused considerable comment, for they were well-behaved and civilized Christian young people. Janie, a rescued twin, and the other boys and girls who had been saved from death, were not savages upon whom a curse rested, but well-trained young people.

Ma Eme, the missionary's old friend and compatriot in this land of evil, was present, and when they met, Mary's eyes filled with tears of thanksgiving, as she remembered those long-ago days when they had worked together. As yet, Ma Eme did not openly embrace Christianity, but she had been influenced by the Gospel's power among her people.

"My dear old friend and almost sister"—thus spoke Mary of Ma Eme. "She made the saving of life so often possible in the early days. It is sad that she would not come out for Christ. She could have been the honored leader of God's work had she risen to it. Hers is a foolish choice. And yet God cannot forget all she was to me and how she helped me in those dark and bloody days."

Hundreds thronged to the spacious church during the commendatory service. Mary had remembered the orgies and drunken brawls during the first days of her work among the people. When the services of rejoicing were finished and the missionary returned to her work, the resident leaders realized what she meant to the natives. They were filled with love and respect for their White Ma.

Shortly after the Akpap visit, Mary received royal recognition for her valuable and unselfish work. She was elected to membership in the Order of the Hospital of St. John of Jerusalem in England and she received its Silver Cross. When Sir Frederick Lugard assumed his duties as Governor-General of Northern and Southern Nigeria, he was impressed by the transformation Mary had wrought among the natives and her success in abolishing cannibalistic customs. Convinced that she deserved recognition, he sent a recommendation which was brought before the King. The King, who was the head of the order, selected her for admission to its noble ranks.

An official-looking document was sent to Duke Town, asking her to accept the honor. With true humility she asked, "Who am I, and what is my distinction that I should have it?" She scarcely knew how to evaluate the honor, and said nothing about it to her friends until the badge arrived. Women wear the Cross on the left shoulder, and it is given only to professing Christians who have outstandingly devoted their work and skill to aid the purpose of the order.

When news came of the honor, the Colonial Office at Duke Town decided that a public ceremony must be held to celebrate this recognition of one so loved by the folk of Calabar and Okoyong. The government launch brought the wizened missionary, now nearly sixty-five, to the coastal city, where the presentation took place at Goldie Hall, which was filled to overflowing with Europeans, boys from the Training Institute and girls from the Edgerley Memorial School.

During the address Mary, overcome by emotion, sat with her head in her hands, and when the time came to reply, she found speech difficult. However, turning to the boys and girls, she told them to be faithful to the government, to be Christians, friends of the mission and followers of the lowly Nazarene.

Writing later to Scotland friends, she said, "Don't think that there is any difference in my designation. I am Mary Mitchell Slessor, nothing more, and none other than the unworthy, unprofitable, but most willing servant of the King of kings. May this be an incentive to work and to be better than ever I have been in the past."

The honor brought wide recognition, and she received congratulations from all over the world. Sir Frederick Lugard sent his "hearty and sincere congratulations and his appreciation of this well-earned reward for her life of heroic sacrifice."

With true missionary humility she declared, "I shall never look the world in the face again until all this blarney and publicity is over. I feel so glad that I can hide here quietly where no one knows about newspapers and missionary records and do my small portion of work out of sight." This was characteristic, for always she was self-effacing. She wrote to her homeland friends that she saw in the honor only "God's goodness to the mission and her fellow workers who were leveling and building and consolidating the work on every side. It is a token that He means to encourage them in the midst of their discouraging circumstances."

The honor inspired Mary to devote herself even more unselfishly to the work she loved so dearly. She was invited to settle at Ikpe, where conditions in the town and the surrounding territory were worse than those in Okoyong when she first canoed to that degraded land. The chiefs told her, "We do not want God-fashion . . . We do not want teachers or churches." Finally, however, in their palavers they agreed to permit schools, "but there must be no interference with our fashions."

Mary declared firmly, "Schools and teachers go with the Gospel. You can't have one without the other. I shall myself hold services wherever I can find a place, even if it is but a roadside shed."

In her "box on wheels," as she termed the cart, she pushed through the jungle, forded streams, climbed hills and went on foot into the regions where the cart could not take her. She persistently opposed the murder of twins, battled heathen practices and secured the chiefs' permission to teach the girls and women.

A government road had been opened as far as Odoro

Ikpe, some miles farther inland, where Mary established temporary mission headquarters. She determined by God's grace to win the chiefs to her side, whatever the cost. She was willing to lay down her life to achieve this purpose. The house had mud floors and small openings in the walls functioned as doors and windows. She borrowed utensils from the bushmen for cooking the native food.

From here she pushed out to small jungle settlements, interviewing chiefs and pleading with the natives. Finally love was victorious and land was given for schoolhouses, but church services were restricted. Mary refused, however, to accept the land under such conditions and subsequently this last objection was removed by the chiefs. Writing to Scottish friends about the triumph, she said, "I am the happiest and most grateful woman in the world."

This necessitated building a house at Odoro Ikpe, where the lack of building materials in abundance made the use of sticks and mud imperative. Mary, however, was not to be deterred, and she accepted the challenge with the same zest which characterized her first building attempt in Okoyong.

Friends insisted that she give up the venture and return to Scotland, but she wrote, "When I do come, it will not be as a week-end visitor or tea visitor, but a barnacle. It is, however, all too alluring. Only one thing can overtop it and that is my duty as put into my hands by my King . . . Put yourself in my place and with an accession of strength since I camped up here, how could you do other than I have done? This came and the strength has come with it, and there must be no more moving till the house is up. What a glorious privilege it all is! I can't think why God has so highly honored and trusted me."

Again she was a pioneer. She supervised the building

of the house, and then began a round of teaching and other
duties which she performed cheerfully.

In August, 1914, rumors reached her that Europe was
rushing headlong into war. This horrified her, for despite
many duties and tedious periods of jungle isolation, she
maintained, through correspondence and periodicals, a keen
interest in world affairs. She realized that this war would
not only bring suffering and horror to many of her dear
friends, but would hamper the work in Calabar.

When the first mail arrived, and she read that war had
been declared, she became unconscious for hours at a time,
but continued for two weeks to carry on her work. The
strain proved too much, and on Friday, January 8, 1915,
she wrote her last words to a friend: "I can't say definitely
whether I shall yet come in March—*if I be spared till then.*"
She sensed that the end was near and that she was soon
to be called home. Recurrent fever laid her low during
the day, but on Sunday, January 10, she conducted her usual
church services. After the meeting, however, she became
unconscious. Doctor Robertson arrived from the Slessor
Hospital at Itu and was able to revive her, but on the
twelfth of January she found it almost impossible to speak.
Her last words were a prayer in Efik, *O Abasi, sana mi yok,*
"O God, release me."

During the night of the twelfth, she was surrounded by
her girls. Janie, now a beautiful black woman, was among
them. Eagerly and tenderly they watched as the night
turned to day. A cock crowed, and one of them said, "Day
must be dawning." Day was indeed dawning—Mary's
eternal day—and at three-thirty on January 13, 1915, when
the world was filled with cannons belching death, the faithful missionary slipped into the eternal harbor of peace.

"Our Mother is dead, and we shall be slaves now that our
Mother is dead," wailed the natives. As the news went

throughout the region, the natives came from Itu and round-about to see the woman whom they called "Everybody's Mother"—*Eka kpukpru owo.* The news was telegraphed to Duke Town that Mary Slessor, the Queen of Okoyong, the White Ma whom Christ had made the conqueror of cannibals, had gone to her eternal rest, and the government launch rushed to Itu, where an English and Efik service was held in honor of this life spent for the Master's glory.

Her body was taken to Duke Town for a memorial service, and the coffin was draped with the British flag, the Union Jack, and carried high on the shoulders of the boat boys, who wore black singlets and mourning loin-cloths, but no caps. At the cemetery, before the service began, old Ma Fuller, Mary's native friend through the years, wailed, "Do not cry, do not cry. Praise God from whom all blessings flow. Ma was a great blessing."

A touching service was conducted at the grave by the Reverend Wilkie and Mr. Rankin, and the natives led in singing "When the Day of Toil Is Done" and "Asleep in Jesus." Teachers from Duke Town lowered the coffin with great solemnity, and gently the men shoveled soft African earth upon Mary's mortal remains. Africa not only received her heart—as it had Livingstone's—but her body as well, for this was her adopted land, where thirty-nine of her sixty-six years had been spent.

Her visible work was terminated. Often she had said, "It isn't Mary Slessor doing anything, but something—God —outside of her altogether uses her, as her small ability allows." Never did she speak of "my plan," but always of "what God wants me to do." Recognizing her shortcomings, she said many times, "I don't half live up to the ideal missionary life. It is not easier to be a saint here than at home. We are very human . . ."

The cry of her soul rang throughout the world:

"We have really no workers to meet all this opened country. Where are the men? Are there no heroes in the making amongst us? No hearts beating high with the enthusiasm of the Gospel? If we cannot meet this new opportunity, our church, to be honest, should stand back and give it to someone else. But, oh, how can our church look at Christ who has given us the privilege of making Calabar history, and say to Him, 'Take it back. Give it to another'?"

She loved the Bible and studied it earnestly. Christ's glorious command had inspired her: "Go ye into all the world, and preach the gospel." Her cry had ever been: "Onward! *I dare not look back!*"

Here is the secret of her success:

"Prayer is the greatest power God has put into our hands for service. Praying is harder work than doing . . . but the dynamic lies that way to advance the kingdom. . . Pray that the power of God may rest upon me, that He may never be disappointed, or find me disobedient to the heavenly vision when He shows the way. Pray that I will make no false moves, but that the Spirit will say, 'Go here' and 'Go there.'"

Mary Slessor's achievements are inspiring evidence of the power of prayer. "I have no idea how and why God has carried me over so many hard places, and made these hordes submit to me . . . except in answer to prayer at home for me. It is all beyond my comprehension. The only way I can explain it is on the ground that I have been prayed for more than most. Pray on—power lies that way."

God was a living presence to Mary Slessor, and Christ was almost visibly near. "When I am out there in the bush, I have often no other one to speak to, and so I just talk to Him," she said in speaking of her conversation with God.

Her labors were finished, but her heroic life continues to be an influence in the African bush and the cannibal jungle. The mud-plastered kirks scattered along the jungle paths are symbols of African redemption. Mary has gone, but her labors will endure until the day dawns.

Printed in the United States of America